YOUR CHOICES, YOUR LIFE

SECOND EDITION

Your Choices, Your Life—Ideas for Living the Adventure Called Life

Published by Next Century Publishing

www.NextCenturyPublishing.com

ISBN: 978-162-9038124

Printed in the United States of America

YOUR CHOICES, YOUR LIFE

SECOND EDITION

IDEAS FOR LIVING THE ADVENTURE CALLED LIFE

DR. WILLIAM S. SVOBODA

NEXT CENTURY
PUBLISHING

Preface

What is worth knowing? What do we need to know to be happy? What are the most useful ideas? What information is valuable enough to pass on formally to the next generation? How can I be a happier and more productive person?

Several years ago, as a college professor investigating the curricula of public schools, these were the most persistent questions that demanded my personal, as well as professional, time. As a result of my investigations into what is worth knowing, I became convinced that the major problem with schools was that what they were trying to teach was most often not worth knowing. Because experts believe that anyone who criticizes is obligated to suggest better alternatives, I started making a list of concepts and skills that would comprise what *I* would teach in schools as basic education. Before I added a new idea to the list of "what is worth knowing," I would try it on for myself. If it did not work for me, I wouldn't advocate it. This very direct form of research proved to be more important than I had expected. Many of my ideas worked. Some of them made profound changes in my life. As my personal life and professional life improved, I couldn't help wondering why I hadn't been taught any of these ideas in my formal education. My life could have been much richer than it was.

Once my list of things worth knowing became larger, I included some of the ideas in the university classes I was teaching. I then developed some new courses built on these ideas. The ideas worked for my students as they had for me. Some of the ideas resulted in profound changes in the lives of my students and their families. Students gained self-confidence, became more productive, gained increased control over their lives in many ways, and reported that they were happier. Many students in my graduate class, however, wondered, as I did, why they had not come in contact with these useful ideas earlier in their formal education. Their lives could have been richer if their basic education had been more about what was *really* worth knowing.

As I continued my research, wrote more ideas into short concept papers, and shared them with students in my classes and others outside the university setting, it became increasingly obvious that these ideas have universal importance. They deal with the basics of life, the things in life that seem to matter the most.

The first edition of this book was used by individuals, parents, teachers (usually middle-school and older), discussion groups, homeschoolers, and counselors. The format of the book is designed to be equally useful to individuals and groups.

Let me tell you about how the book is written and how you might use it. This is deliberately a short book. I have observed that many large books don't get read or even started because people don't feel they have the time to devote to that much reading. Each of the 36 concepts (except one) is also deliberately very short and concise. I've observed that many people don't want to sit through 20 pages to find ideas that could be communicated in two pages. Each concept is what you might otherwise call a "big idea" or a "useful idea." Each chapter stands alone. There is no sequence intended. You can read the chapters in any order. I have tried to use universal examples to explain how the ideas work and how you might use them to gain more control over your life.

You might find it helpful to use the book to discuss the ideas as a family or you might use the ideas from the book in a more formal class, club, or study group. The format should be helpful in promoting any type of intellectual group activity. Because of their short length, the chapters will more likely be read prior to the meeting or class. The concise format should help focus the discussion on the ideas and the applications of those ideas to the lives of the individuals in the group. The discussion questions and activities are designed to help individuals or group leaders understand and apply the ideas.

These ideas have worked for me and many others. These are ideas to be explored. They are possibilities to be investigated. They are insights to be considered. Accept those that you feel will help you become *what* you want to become and *who* you want to become. Refine and modify some of the ideas to make them better for your particular needs. They are for you to use and are written with life application in mind. A good idea that is not used is really no better than a lack of ideas. There are many interesting, provocative, and useful ideas here for you either to use or reject. Do so as you see fit.

It is *your choice*.

It is *your life*.

ABOUT THE AUTHOR

Dr. Bill Svoboda earned his doctorate from the University of Kansas. He taught in the public schools in Kansas and Puerto Rico. He also taught in higher education at Kansas University, Missouri University, the University of Puerto Rico, the College of National Education in Tanzania, Africa, and Arizona State University. In 2000, Dr. Svoboda retired as professor and dean from Arizona State University and began serving as Chief Operations Officer for the West Valley Child Crisis Center. He is also the founder and principal of PotentialMAX, a company designed to maximize individual and organizational potential.

Dr. Svoboda has held several positions throughout his professional career, including lecturer, education officer, professor, Director of Social Studies Resource Center, Director of Economics Education, Faculty Program Coordinator, Acting Director of Education and Human Services, Interim Director of Education, and Dean of the College of Education and consultant.

Before becoming an educator, Bill worked as a farm laborer, plasterer, painter, construction laborer, railroad breakout, mobile home salesman, and soil compaction tester for an engineering company.

Bill has written or edited dozens of articles, monographs, book chapters, and teaching resources. He has also written a citizenship text for junior and senior high school, *The Missouri*

Citizen. His childhood hero was Leonardo da Vinci, and he has been researching a fundamental question for the last several decades. That question is, "What's Worth Knowing?" Some of the most important answers to that question constitute this book.

Bill's hobbies include painting, sketching, cut glass, writing, reading, traveling, exercise, and especially "people watching." Although he considers himself a citizen of the planet, he currently lives in Arizona. He has two daughters, four grandchildren and four great-grandchildren. His favorite quote is attributed to Mahatma Gandhi, "Live as if you were to die tomorrow. Learn as if you were to live forever."

Table of Contents

CHAPTER 1

You Are the Sum of Your Habits

If you think about it you are, in large part, a sum of all of your habits. We can define habits as *behaviors that we repeat on a regular basis*. This might be a good time to think of the various habits you have and how they affect your life.

- **NUTRITION:** What do you normally eat? How much? How often? Do you eat to live or live to eat? Is your daily diet based on nutrition science or more on just what you like?

- **EXERCISE:** What kind? How often? What intensity? Are you strong enough to do your daily tasks? Are you happy with the way you look?

- **MENTAL OUTLOOK:** Are you usually positive? Do you customarily focus on the good in your life?

- **GOAL-SETTING:** Do you set clearly identifiable goals toward which you are consistently moving, or are you too busy "getting somewhere" to take the time to think about *where* you're going and *if* you should really be going there?

- **APPROACH TO HEALTH:** Are your health habits based on your accepting the responsibility for your health, or do you just do whatever feels good and leave your health to the doctor?

- **YOUR APPROACH TO LIFE IN GENERAL:** Are you a participator in life, or are you primarily a spectator? Do you play or do you watch? Are you a problem-solver or a complainer? Are you in control of your life or do events, circumstances, and other people control you?

- **INFORMATION:** Do you ask questions and seek information that can make your life better, or do you spend most of your time watching television in order to forget about the part of your life that isn't as good as you would like it to be? Is your free time spent mostly to entertain yourself?

- **SAFETY:** Are you in the habit of using the seatbelt in a car, wearing a helmet on a bicycle, obeying the speed limit, and generally behaving in order to keep you and others from being needlessly injured; or are you more likely to do whatever pleases you at the moment without regard for the safety of others or yourself?

- **ENTERTAINMENT:** What are you learning from the kinds of entertainment you usually choose? Will they have an overall positive impact on your life, or will they have negative consequences? What kinds of values are taught by the television programs you watch or the music to which you listen? How much of your free time is spent entertaining yourself?

16

- **OUTLOOK ABOUT PEOPLE:** How do you think about other people? Do you see people as generally good, worthy, ambitious, and to be trusted; or do you see them as devious, lazy, and untrustworthy? How does this influence your treatment of other people and how they perceive you?

- **HOW YOU TALK TO YOURSELF:** How do you usually talk to yourself (or think to yourself) when something goes wrong? What do you think to yourself when you look in the mirror? What do you think to yourself when someone criticizes something about you or pays you a compliment?

- **GETTING JOBS DONE:** Do you normally start at the first chance you get and finish in a reasonable amount of time? Do you wait until the last minute to start a task? Would you describe yourself as a procrastinator?

There are many other categories of habits, and certainly many other subcategories, that could be listed under the areas of life above. The point here is that you have many different behaviors that you repeat with enough regularity to call them personal habits. These personal habits, if added together, comprise a major portion of who you are.

This would be a great time to list and evaluate your overall habits. You may start with the list of categories above and add to it as you see fit. It is often valuable to have others to help you create your list because you may not be fully aware of some of your habits. Be open-minded, honest, and thorough in developing this list of personal habits.

When you have finished the list, it should represent you, or at least a substantial part of you, personally and professionally. You will find some habits of which you are proud and are helping you to reach your potential. These comprise the valuable, competent, desirable person you are; however, because none of us is perfect (except maybe the author), you will undoubtedly also find some habits of which you are not so proud. These are the habits that are keeping you from reaching your full potential; believe it or not, they are threatening your future. These undesirable habits represent your opportunity to change positively, to gain more control over your life, and to grow even more. So what can you do about these undesirable habits?

Never try to quit a bad habit. Allow me to explain. If you found some habits that you determined to be working against your best interests, the first thing that you'd be likely to do is vow to quit or stop that habit. The very fact that you use the negative term of "quit" makes your attempt to change that much more unlikely. For example, many people want to quit smoking cigarettes, stop eating non-nutritious and fattening foods, quit watching mindless television programs, stop procrastinating, quit being so negative about their lives, stop being a couch potato, or quit looking for the worst in people. Sounds perfectly reasonable, right? Not necessarily. So why shouldn't you try to quit bad habits like these? Here's why.

Firstly, you think in pictures. Your mind processes information best when you have the clearest mental picture possible. Secondly, your mind cannot picture the negative of something. For example, if you close your eyes and think, "I do not see a red beach ball floating in the middle of the swimming pool," you automatically visualize the red ball floating in the pool. You don't, however, visualize the "not" in the sentence. The most vivid impression in your mind is that of the clearest picture expressed in the sentence or thought: the red ball in the swimming pool.

This leads to the third reason why we don't want to think about quitting a bad habit. What we think about tends to come about. What you think about is a good predicator of how you will behave and the kind of person you are and will become. If you see yourself as a stupid person, you will tend to act like a stupid person. If you think of yourself as a bright, energetic person who is capable of doing just about anything, you will be much more likely to have a productive and satisfying life. So how do these three reasons add up?

If (a) your mind thinks best in pictures, (b) it cannot picture negatives, and (c) what you think about is what is most likely to happen, then you don't want to think in terms of quitting bad habits. "I will not eat cherry pie with ice cream on top," is an example of the kind of the quitting-a-habit approach you don't want to use. Your mind records "cherry pie with ice cream on top," but it doesn't record the word "not." What just happened to you when you read the sentence, "I will not eat cherry pie with ice cream on top," the first time? Didn't you see in your mind the picture of the cherry pie with ice cream on top? Was the ice cream vanilla or chocolate? Maybe you even felt your mouth begin to salivate as you anticipated the slightly bitter taste of the cherries in contrast to the sweet and creamy taste of the ice cream. Maybe you felt the warmth of the pie and the contrast with the coolness of the ice cream—probably vanilla, right? Every time you told yourself that you were not going to eat cherry pie with ice cream on top, you would get a vivid mental picture of eating cherry pie with ice cream on top! That vivid mental picture just increases the chance that the negative habit you are trying to avoid will happen because what you *think* about tends to *come* about. Be careful!

Always picture in your mind the habit that you want to develop. In contrast to the negative example above, you would positively think, "I will eat some delicious fresh fruit for dessert." You wouldn't "quit smoking" but would "put the purest air available in your lungs." You wouldn't think, "Stop watching football on television," but would think, "Get off the couch and play some football with friends." Always concentrate your thinking on the habit you want to make—not on the one you want to break.

Program yourself to go to a "good habit" that will replace the "bad habit."

QUESTIONS

1. Do you believe that a person is, in large part, the sum of his or her habits?

2. Do you believe that you have more "good" habits than "bad" habits?

3. Do you believe that who you are is determined, in large part, by your habits?

4. What three habits do you have that you are most proud of?

5. What three habits do you have that you would like to change?

6. If you would like to change these undesirable habits, why haven't you changed them yet?

7. Why does the author caution you not to try to quit a bad habit?

8. What habits are there in the world that you believe we would be better off not having? For example, the habit of settling disagreements through violence is a habit that most people think we would be better off not having.

9. What are some habits in the world that you believe should be practiced more widely? For example, the habit of doing

physical exercise on a regular basis is a habit that health experts would agree should be practiced more widely.

10. If someone had a habit that was harmful to him or her, would you tell the person about it?

11. If someone saw that you had a habit that was harmful to you, would you want the person to tell you about it?

ACTIVITIES

1. Take the time to write down some of your habits under each of the categories listed in the first part of this chapter. For example, what habits do you have under the categories of nutrition, safety, and getting jobs done? Which habits are good for you? Which ones do you think you might be better off replacing? Do you notice any patterns concerning your habits?

2. Choose one of the habits that you feel is not good for you and picture in your mind the behavior you will use to replace it. What does your mental picture look like?

3. With a partner or any small group, share the habit that you do not want to continue, then share your mental picture of the positive behavior with which you want to replace it. Help each other clarify the picture to ensure that you are doing it correctly.

CHAPTER 2

Worry Is a Waste

Worry! Worry! Worry! One of the most wasteful things you can do is to worry. Worry doesn't help anything, and it wastes your time and your energy. Worry is nothing more than thinking about things that you don't want to happen in the future or that you didn't want to happen in the past. When you are worrying about the future or the past, you are wasting your present. Your present is the time in which you really live. Another way of saying this is that you can waste the great value of your present life by thinking about what went wrong in your past and what you are afraid will go wrong in the future.

Worrying about the past is terribly wasteful because the past is gone and thinking about what went wrong in your past life does not help anything. What does it help to dwell on the time when you were embarrassed giving a speech in front of your English class? Does it help to continue to brood over the time when your father yelled at you for something you did not do? Does it help anything to remember when your pet dog was killed by a car? There are simply no good reasons to think about the undesirable events in your past over and over, but many people do. Do you?

Of course, you can learn from unpleasant past experiences by thinking of ways you can behave differently in similar situations in the future. For example, you might learn that you can lessen your stress when you give a speech if you are interested in the topic and you have note cards to keep your speech organized. You can use this discovery from the past to help you in the future; however, this is quite different from mulling over how embarrassed you were when you forgot your speech, the other students who were laughing at you, and the teacher who was criticizing you for not preparing properly. The best way to deal with past failure is to learn something from it that will be useful in the future, and then forget it. It's over.

Worrying about the past is the same as hitting yourself in the head with a baseball bat, except that it hurts on the inside instead of the outside. If you must think about the past, then think about the good things that happened to you, the great friends, the beautiful sights and sounds, and all of the successes you have had. And you have had successes.

Worrying about the future is even worse than worrying about the past. When you worry about the future, you think about what you don't want to happen. This is different from planning for the future. When you plan for the future, you think about what you can do to make the future happen the way you want it to happen. For example, if you knew that you were going to give a speech, you would plan your topic, find information about the topic, maybe find an appropriate joke to tell, practice the speech to be sure it would fit in the time allowed, and so on. This is quite different from what you would do if you were worrying about giving the speech. If you were worrying, you would be thinking of how you might forget part of your speech, how the audience might not laugh at your joke or might be bored and go to sleep as you talk, or how you might drop your note cards in the middle of your presentation. Planning how to make things go right makes sense, but worrying about what can go wrong is, at best, a waste of time and energy.

Thinking about what you don't want to happen can be even worse than a simple waste of your energy and time. It can actually program you to fail. That is, when you worry about something, you are actually increasing the possibility that the thing you don't want to happen will happen. This is because what we think about tends to come about. The more we think about something, be it good or bad, the more likely it is to happen. In the example from above, the worrying or thinking about all the things that you don't want to happen is actually programming you to have those things happen. The more you worry, the more vivid are the mental images of your forgetting, the audience not laughing and being bored, and you dropping your notes. When you actually step up to the podium to give your speech, some of the most vivid mental images you will have are of the worst things that could happen to you. You are now more likely to forget, to tell your joke hesitantly because you "know" the audience will not laugh, to deliver the speech without your usual enthusiasm because your mind already is programmed that the audience will be bored, and your hands can't wait for the right moment to fulfill your mental image of dropping your notes. This is why worrying about the future is even worse than worrying about the past.

From now on, you will think about how things will go right. You know that it does not help anything to think about what you didn't want to have happen in your past. You know it is even worse to think about what you don't want to have happen in the future because you are actually making it more likely to happen. You know that it makes sense to learn from the past by analyzing what you can do better next time, but you know that once you have done that, the negative past is best forgotten. You know that planning for the future includes considering how to overcome negative possibilities, but you also know that thinking about what you want to have happen is the basis of being successful. What you think about tends to come about, so let your mind create mental pictures of things going well.

Before your speech, visualize yourself calm, alert, entertaining, and looking at an audience that is attentive and appreciative of what you have to say.

Maybe your speech should be about how worrying is a waste!

QUESTIONS

1. Do you believe that worry is a waste? Why or why not?

2. What are some alternatives to worrying about the past or thinking about undesirable things that have happened to you? More specifically, if you must think about something in your past, how can you make it beneficial rather than a wasteful use of your time?

3. Have you ever worried excessively about something that happened in the past? For example, did you ever lie in bed unable to sleep as you thought over and over again about something bad that happened to you? Did it help anything to rerun the event over and over in your mind? Could this just be a habit you have gotten into? How might you replace this habit?

4. Using the definitions of "worry" presented in this chapter, do you think it is ever useful to worry about the past or the future?

5. Do you suppose animals other than humans worry?

6. What would be the worst possible outcome you could think of that would be the result of worrying about the past?

7. What would be the worst possible outcome you could think of that would be the result of worrying about the future?

ACTIVITIES

1. Explain in your own words why it is so wasteful to worry about the future. Use the definition that worrying about the future is nothing more than thinking about something negative that you don't want to have happen. Keep in mind that what you think about tends to come about. Use an original example involving people about your own age.

2. Write a short description of the difference between worrying about the future and planning for the future. Use original examples.

3. Can you illustrate any of the ideas in this chapter using cartoons, drawings, or any other visual medium?

4. Contrast worrying about the past with learning from the past; use examples that would be easily understood by someone else.

CHAPTER 3

You Are in Control of Your Happiness

You are in control of your happiness. You can control your thoughts, and the way you think determines how happy you will be. Every day you experience events and people in your life, and you interpret those experiences. Your interpretation of these events and people results in your emotions such as happiness, sadness, anger, frustration, elation, or joy. For example, events such as losing a job, death of a loved one, losing a pet, or getting a "bad" grade in school will be interpreted in negative terms by most people. How would *you* react to each of these events? Your reactions would probably be non-happy emotions such as worry, fear, sadness, and stress.

On the other hand, what kinds of emotions would you expect when people win a million dollars, fall in love with a fantastic person who loves them in return, are offered a job that they dreamed of getting, or get a near-perfect score on a major test? How would you feel about these events if they happened to you? You would probably feel elated, joyful, delighted, and quite happy.

Note, however, that any of the events above that are interpreted as positive could be interpreted as negative, and vice versa. For example, if you were fired from a job, you would probably interpret that as negative, but you could also view it positively as an opportunity to try a new job, have some extra variety in your life, move to a different location in the country, or perhaps to re-evaluate your life and what you are going to do with it. On the other hand, if you are offered the job of your dreams, you could view it with negative terms. You might still feel stress because you are unsure of the new situation, or you might be worried that you won't get the pay or benefits you expect. You might be apprehensive that your new supervisor will not be as understanding as the one you work with now.

The outcomes of ways we interpret events are our emotions. If you remember formulas better, then you could write: **events you experience + your interpretation of the events = your emotions.** The events you and I experience do not have automatic human emotions tied to them. The events we experience simply exist in nature with no values placed on them other than the values we give them. Nature doesn't judge good or bad. For example, when you see a film in which a fox is chasing a rabbit, you probably wish for the rabbit to escape. Few people wish for the fox to catch the rabbit even though it is natural for foxes to eat rabbits. If the fox does not kill and eat, the fox will die. In the natural food chain, the rabbit is food for the fox; this is not "good" or "bad" as far as nature is concerned (note that "nature" and "natural" come from the same root word); it is just natural. We, in our culture, however, have learned to value rabbits more than foxes, so we feel sad to see the "cute little bunny" get eaten by the "nasty old fox." We could just as easily be happy that the beautiful fox will be able to live and feed its young after eating the overabundance of near-rodents that destroy so much of the farmer's crops. Can you

32

think of some of the ways you learned your ideas about rabbits and foxes?

In the same way, we usually feel bad when we see a snake eating a mouse or a frog. Of course, our emotions change a great deal when we are in a restaurant and we happen to like rabbit stew or breaded frog legs. We interpret mice quite differently if they escape the mouth of a snake but then get into our house. Also, we can see the snake as a frightening, ugly creature to be slashed to bits at the first opportunity, or we can see it as a beautiful, graceful, and shy reptile that has as much right as any other creature to live on this planet. Can you remember where you got your ideas about snakes? Can you see how your interpretation based on your previous learning about snakes results in your emotions about snakes when you see them? The snake is a natural being and only exists doing what snakes are supposed to do in the scheme of things. It is your interpretation that puts a positive or negative value on it and results in your emotion of fear and loathing or fascination and awe.

Perhaps the most vivid example of how our interpretation of events determines our emotional state is the event we call death. There are cultures and individuals who have been taught that death is a terrible event where a person is taken away forever and that grief, sorrow, and pain are the emotions that are appropriate and expected of relatives and friends. Other cultures and individuals have been taught to interpret death as one step in the evolution of life (sort of a necessary part of the natural recycling process) to be accepted as inevitable and natural without expecting deep emotional responses. Still, other cultures and individuals seek out the celebration of the life of the deceased. It is a time for remembering the person and his or her accomplishments, friends, events, and the good times in the person's life. It is a positive event of celebration rather than a negative one of grief. The same common event of death can result in many different emotions, depending on the way we interpret it.

Every emotion you have is the result of your interpretation. The events didn't cause your emotion; how you thought about the events caused your emotion. You can be a happier person by consciously making it a habit to interpret the events in your life in the most realistic and positive ways possible.

Look for the silver lining—and the beautiful snake.

QUESTIONS

1. Make a list of all of the emotions you might have over a lifetime—25 to 30 will do.

2. What is your reaction to the idea that "emotions are nothing more than thoughts, and because you can control what you think, you can control your emotions"? This statement refers to the formula: events you experience + your interpretation of the events = your emotions. Do you agree or disagree? What examples from real life can you use to support your position?

3. Remember the examples (the fox and the rabbit, the snake and the frog, and death) and how you interpreted these things through your beliefs to be bad or good? Think of an event in your life that was sad or unhappy for you. What beliefs or values have you been taught to cause you to feel that the event was sad or unhappy? What beliefs would you have to have been taught to make the event seem like a good or even happy one?

4. React to the statement that reads, "You can be a happier person by consciously making it a habit to interpret events in your life in the most positive ways possible." Do you believe that makes sense? Why or why not? Give real-life examples to support your position.

5. What if you looked for the worst in everything that happened to you? What kind of person do you think you would be? Do you think you would have many friends? What kinds of facial features do you think you would have?

6. What do you think would happen if people you knew interpreted what happened to them in the most negative way? Is this the kind of place where you would want to live? What if they did the opposite and had only positive, realistic interpretations?

7. Imagine that you have a best friend who is forced to move to a distant city because of a fantastic, once-in-a-lifetime job offer. How many interpretations of that event can you think of and what emotions would you have?

ACTIVITIES

1. Individually or in your group, brainstorm a list of events that are usually interpreted as sad or bad. Some examples would be losing a contest, having a close friend move away, having a relative die, or seeing hundreds of starving people on the news. Now take the events that are usually interpreted in a negative way and see how you could interpret them in a more positive, or at least a non-negative, way. For example, you could be happy that your close friend moved away because she will like the location better, have new opportunities, have more variety in her life, and you can still keep in contact with her by phone, email, or writing.

2. Individually or in your group, brainstorm a list of events that are usually interpreted as being happy or good. Some examples would be your favorite professional ball team winning five games in a row, finding out that you just inherited a new sporty car just like the one you always dreamed of owning, or being invited to a party by the most popular member of the opposite sex whom you know. Now take each of the events that are usually interpreted in a positive way and see how you can interpret them in a negative or less positive way. For example, the inheritance of the car means that someone in your family died, and that is probably sad for you in some way; you'll also probably be stressed about having to pay for upkeep on the car that could, in turn, cause you to work more or have to get another job that would take away time from other things that you love to do.

3. Make a list of at least three to five things you could do right now to gain more control over the amount of happiness you have in your life. Share your ideas with others. Add to your list behaviors you have learned from the lists of others. Make copies of your list and put them in places where you will be reminded of the new habits you are developing to gain more control over your happiness.

CHAPTER 4

How Do You Talk to Yourself When Things Don't Go Right?

No matter how much you are in control of your life, you will encounter events that don't go right. Your car gets banged up. Your checking account becomes overdrawn. Your vacation has to be postponed because the dog needs a tonsillectomy. Someone in your family gets sick. Someone dies. There are lots of "bad" things that can happen to you. Bad stuff happens in life. How you react is crucial.

A major part of your reaction to a negative event is how you think or talk to yourself about it. For example, some unknowing person carelessly backs into your new car in the parking lot and puts a large dent in the center. How would you react? You can become hysterical and think and talk in catastrophic terms such as, "I hate the idiot who hit my car. I loved that car. Even if they fix it perfectly, I'll know it has been wrecked and will never enjoy it again." You would be making a final decision that the car would be forever worthless to you. A relatively simple and easily-remedied dent in the car is made into a tragedy by the way you think about it. Not only is the event blown out of proportion, but it is also stated in an absolutely and eternally negative form. If you think this way, you will hate your car for as long as you keep it, regardless of how well it can be repaired. If you were to make this catastrophic type of thinking a habit, you would be in for a very miserable life.

What would happen if you were to react in a more realistic way when confronted with this hypothetical "fender bender"? You could think something like, "I'm not happy about this and it's going to be inconvenient. I'll have to call the insurance company and get the car fixed. It is unfortunate that it happened, but it isn't a big enough deal to get upset about." Note that in this case you'd be expressing your justifiable unhappiness, but you put the incident into perspective and moved forward with your life. This realistic approach to dealing with the "bad" situation is based on an objective perspective that assigns a temporary status to the unpleasant situation, emphasizes action to deal with the immediate incident, and implies that life will go on despite the temporary setback. If you can make this realistic type of thinking a habit, you are much more likely to be happy and productive in the long-term because you keep your problems in proper perspective.

The following terms represent the kind of thinking that you would be doing if you were thinking in the catastrophic rather than the realistic modes.

- **CATASTROPHIC SELF-TALK**

   It's horrible!

   My life is ruined!

   Things will never be right!

   I'll never recover from this!

   It's a disaster!

I'm destroyed!

What a calamity!

It's a tragedy!

I'll be miserable from now on!

I'm completely overwhelmed!

It's final and fatal!

I'll never love again!

This is a downfall I can't survive!

I'm so depressed; I don't know what to do!

I give up!

I have to live with this the rest of my life!

- **REALISTIC SELF-TALK**

It's unfortunate…

It's inconvenient…

It's a temporary setback…

This will slow my progress, but…

It's a temporary frustration…

Okay…now what's my next step?

That's unlucky…

It's a bad situation, but…

That's upsetting, but…

It will be more difficult than I expected, but…

It's unsettling, but…

It's awkward, but…

It's annoying, but…

41

It's natural to have failure once in a while...

It's going to be burdensome for a while...

Do you use any of these terms? Into which category do you usually fit? Do you sometimes think in catastrophic terms and other times in realistic terms? If yes, under what circumstances do you think in these different ways?

In summary, how we mentally talk to ourselves in undesirable situations can be the difference between immobility, anxiety, stress, and possible depression on one hand, and purposeful action, composure, hope, and problem-solving on the other. Catastrophic thinking is characterized by overreaction, overly negative perspective, and negative finality. Realistic thinking accepts an undesirable situation as unfortunate, but temporary, employs a perspective of realistic optimism, emphasizes that life must go on.

Understand that the predicament can get better.

QUESTIONS

1. What was the latest bad thing that happened to you? How did you react? Was your self-talk mostly catastrophic or realistic?

2. What are the main differences between a catastrophic reaction to a "bad" event and a realistic reaction to the same negative effect?

3. What are some terms you usually use in your self-talk when things don't go the way you want? Are they more catastrophic or more realistic?

4. What do you see as being wrong with catastrophic self-talk?

5. Do you think that realistic self-talk is better for you than catastrophic self-talk? Why?

6. Think of someone you know fairly well. Does he or she usually react in catastrophic or realistic ways? Provide examples.

7. Can you add to the list of terms that represent catastrophic thinking and realistic thinking?

ACTIVITIES

1. Create a drawing, painting, cartoon, or some other visual illustration of a person using catastrophic self-talk after a bad event in his or her life. Now, using the same situation, illustrate the person using realistic self-talk.

2. Divide the group or class into smaller groups of three to five. Have each group create a realistic bad situation that could happen to someone like them. Have them write down the situation on a piece of paper, and then have them exchange papers with another group. Ask each group to determine how a person would react to the situation using catastrophic self-talk and then how he might react using realistic self-talk. Have the smaller groups share their reactions with the total group. Write the characteristics of both catastrophic and realistic self-talk in a conspicuous place so that each of their reactions can be compared. Based on these criteria, suggest improvements that might make the reactions more consistent.

CHAPTER 5

Another Place to Practice: In Your Head

Practicing is the key to better performance. Musicians practice with their musical instruments to improve their performance. Basketball players practice shooting, defense, and passing to improve their performance. If you knew you had to give a speech, you would probably practice it to increase your chances of doing well. Although practice is most often thought of as being used in athletic events, you can use it to prepare for just about any kind of activity. We practice by performing the actual activity we want to improve. That is, we practice using the musical instrument we will play in the band, we go to the gym to shoot free throws in preparation for the game, and we actually perform our speech to someone in the family before we give it to the class, the business meeting, or at church.

There is another place to practice: in your head. Deliberately practicing something in your mind exactly as you want it to happen can be called positive mental practice. This means that you can practice anything you can picture in your mind. Take a second and mentally picture writing your name on a white sheet of paper with a black pen that has blue ink. When you do it, close your eyes and make a mental picture of how it looks and feels as you write your name. Now do it.

What did you see and feel? Did you see mentally what

you see when you actually write your name? Did you feel the muscles in your hand actually moving as you wrote your name? Perhaps you could even smell the ink from the pen or hear the faint sound of the pen point as it went across the paper. Now change your mental picture and visualize yourself riding down a street on a ten-speed bicycle. What do you see? What do your muscles feel? Can you feel how you are balancing the bike to keep it upright? Can you feel and hear the bumps in the street as you run over them? Now let's use this mental picturing as a way to practice.

Before you do any more visualizing, take time to think of something you do that you would like to do better. This can be a skill such as hitting a ball, singing a song, running a race, or anything in which you need to perform some task. This will be the performance you will improve with your mental practice. Here are some hints that can make your mental practice more efficient.

Make your mental picture as clear and vivid as you possibly can. See the colors, shapes, and shading. Hear the sounds, smell the odors, feel your muscles move, feel the cold or heat.

You can do your mental practice anywhere you feel comfortable. Most people find that they practice best in a quiet area or an area that has white noise, which is a sound that is loud enough to block out distracting sounds but is not distracting in and of itself. Many find that softly-played chamber music and calming new age music are both especially appropriate. *The main idea here is that you do not want distractions to interfere with your mental practice.*

Find a good time to practice. Although you can do mental practice at any time, most people who practice it find that it is especially effective just before they go to sleep at night and first thing when they awaken in the morning; however, don't feel confined only to these times. The most important thing is that you *do* practice and that you practice at a time that is convenient and most comfortable for you.

The more you practice, the more you can improve. Short-term excellence can result from naturally-inherited ability, but long-term excellence always involves dedication to practice. Most people find that having a scheduled time to practice gets them into the habit of mentally practicing a certain amount each day or each week. This is an individual decision based on many things such as time available, how long the mental practice takes, how distracting the surroundings are, how important the performance is to them, among other things. *In general, practice as often as you feel you can without becoming bored or burned out.*

An obviously good time to practice mentally is just before the event or performance. You can visualize yourself doing the behavior exactly as you want it to be done. In your mind, you see and feel your body perform just the way you want it to, then you immediately do the actual performance. This is exactly what many professional athletes do. Many of the record-breaking performances you see in events such as the Olympics are the result of this mental practice just before the athletes perform. Next time you have the opportunity, watch how the performers often stand seemingly lost in their own thoughts. That is when they are visualizing how they will successfully perform that event. You can do it, too.

Mental practice is just like actual practice in that you need to practice doing things correctly. If you visualize yourself hitting a golf ball with poor form in the swing of the club, you will be practicing a poor swing. The results when you are on the golf course will be just as bad as if you had actually practiced hitting the balls with poor form. *Remember that practice*

47

tends to make behaviors permanent. Practice does not make perfect. Make sure that what you practice is how it should be done. Take lessons, watch experts, buy CDs, read books, and so on, to find out how to do it correctly.

Be sure that you have practiced the skill (especially if it involves body movement and dexterity) by actually doing it correctly several times before you practice it mentally. This is important because you want to "feel" the correct way of doing the behavior throughout your body as you visualize the behavior being done exactly as you want it to be done. You can't mentally "feel" it unless you have experienced it before. For example, a pole vaulter would not benefit much from mental practice unless he had actually vaulted and knew how it felt to successfully complete a jump.

Think positively and practice positively. Another key to effective mental practice is practicing how it should happen ideally. You do not think about how things could go wrong unless you are practicing how you would react positively to that negative occurrence. For example, if you were going to give a speech, you would want to practice mentally how you would give your presentation perfectly; however, you might also practice what you would do in the event that you forgot some part of your speech or that you didn't get the laugh that you expected from your opening joke. Keep in mind that practice tends to make permanent. It works just as well for permanent *negative* as it does for permanent *positive*. Perhaps the best way of dealing with this is to get into the habit of thinking in the positive all the time.

Positive mental practice can be an excellent supplement to a hands-on practice schedule for performers of any kind. In fact, many people use it as part of their normal schedule of practice but plan their mental practice for more convenient times. Mental practice is especially useful when regular practice is not possible because of weather conditions, inability to use facilities, or when injuries or illness prevent the actual physical practice. Depending on individual preferences, mental practice can be used at just about any time or place.

Visualizing yourself being successful is a very good habit.

QUESTIONS

1. Does mental practice make sense to you?

2. What are some activities in which you regularly participate? Do you regularly practice for these activities, or should you practice more? In what ways do you practice before the actual event or performance? Would you be willing to try mental practice?

3. What would be the best environment for you to use mental practice? Describe that environment. Is such an environment available to you? If not, can you create one in some way? How close can you come to this environment?

4. When is the best time for you to engage in mental practice? Can you do it just prior to your participation in the actual activity? Can you find a regular time to do your mental practice just as you find time to do your physical practice?

5. Why is it always important to practice the *positive* part of the performance?

6. A baseball player is in a slump. His batting average is much lower than usual. He goes to you, the coach, and says he has videotapes of when he was hitting really well and some of his recent very poor hitting. How would you advise the player to use the tapes? Does anything in the chapter apply?

ACTIVITIES

1. The author states, "Short-term excellence can result from naturally-inherited ability, but long-term excellence always involves dedication to practice." Based on your experience, do you think that is a valid statement? Why or why not?

2. Ask members of the group to help you find ways to measure to what degree your mental practice is helping you improve a performance you have chosen. You might need to consult someone outside your group who knows how to conduct a research experiment and who is willing to help you. Remember that you want to measure your performance before you start mental practice and then again after you have been using mental practice for some time. For example, a famous experiment used the activity of shooting free throws and compared how many were made before and after different kinds of practice.

3. How could the old saying, "Practice makes perfect," be considered incorrect? Write out your answer or answers and then compare among the members of your group.

4. Explain in your own words why it is important to have actually practiced the performance correctly at some time prior to your mental practice. Be very clear and use vivid examples.

5. Now that you know more about mental practice, what are some activities or performances that you could or should start practicing using the mental practice approach? This would be in addition to practice you already do.

52

6. If you were the coach of an athletic team, how could you use mental practice to improve your players' performance? Have members of the group who have interest in the same athletic events work together. Have them develop a list of all the mental practice applications they can think of that are related to their sport. Have the different sport groups share their applications with other groups. Based on feedback from the other groups, each group should refine the applications they used.

CHAPTER 6

Making Lists: Some Suggestions to Make Them Work for You

I meant to do that. I just forgot. It slipped my mind. I can't remember everything. I thought I would remember. These are the often-repeated "excuses" of people who miss appointments, important meetings, and obligations of all sorts. If this sounds familiar, there is a simple remedy: make lists of what you need to do. Whether you use pencil and paper or an electronic device, the use of lists can increase your productivity, decrease your stress, and give you the reputation of someone who can be counted on. Here are some suggestions that might make your use of lists more helpful.

A list is simply writing down things that you want to remember. That's it. You might write down what you need to buy when you go to the grocery store, what you want to take on a trip, or the different places you need to stop as you do several kinds of shopping. Perhaps you also write down daily activities or jobs that you do not want to forget. It is a good idea. Few people can remember everything. A characteristic of successful people is that they are organized, and lists are basic to organization and planning.

A list is not a listing of activities that must be done every day. Many people have unwittingly assumed lists are daily agendas that must be slavishly followed and completed each day. This type of thinking can make a list into a negative stress-producer rather than a simple tool of memory. If you think about it at all, you can see how foolish it is to believe that the lists you write each day will equal the time you have to complete them that day. You know that there will be days when you will have things left on your list because you had a large number of tasks or because the tasks were so time-consuming that you simply couldn't complete all of them. That is reality. To think that we can complete all of our lists every day is not reality. This misinterpretation of the use of lists is the main reason many people don't utilize them.

Prioritize the items on your list. Although the primary reason for making lists is to have a written memory of things you need to do, another reason is that you can prioritize those things and become more efficient. This means that you indicate the items on your list in their order of importance. You complete the most important item on your list first. Then you complete the next most important item. This keeps you more efficient than those of us who work on the easier items on our list first regardless of how important they are.

Start off your list with a quick task that will get the ball rolling. Despite what is said above, there may be times when you want to finish a quick and easy item on your list first thing in the morning so that you can check off something from the list. This gives some people a good feeling of success and encourages them to go on to the more difficult but higher-priority items on the list. Another way to get a quick start on the list is to leave one of the items that was completed on the list from the day before and not mark it off so the first thing in the morning you can check it off and have a running start at your day. Most people don't use these tactics, but you might want to try them to see if they help you get started by telling your subconscious that you have already had a success and are ready to continue your trend.

Make and prioritize your list the day before. This list then represents the tasks and problems that will occupy much of your next day. People who do this find that they have the evening and night to think about completing those tasks. Much of this planning and problem-solving is done consciously, but much of it may also be done by the subconscious. This strategy works and should be given a trial. Planning the night before also gives many people more peace of mind because they know that they have direction to their work the next day and don't have to worry about planning first thing in the morning.

Don't worry about the items that are left on your list at the end of the day. Sometimes there will be a deadline that you must complete and you may have to work late to finish. This usually happens when you are informed of a deadline too late to plan for it in your priorities. The main thing is to remember that you should feel good about the items on your list that you have finished and not worry about the ones you did not complete. If you have prioritized your list and done the most important things first, you can be proud of what you have completed. You have not only completed a quantity of items, but they were also the most important items. The ones you did not complete were the least important. You not only worked hard, but you worked *smart*.

The unfinished items simply carry over to the next day's list. These will not necessarily be the highest priorities for the next day. You will want to make a new list for each day that incorporates both the items left from the previous day and those that you need to add. You then prioritize all the items on your list for that day. There may be some items that carry over for several days. In some cases, you might discover that they are out of date or were not worth doing.

The simple technique of making a daily list of things you need to get done, and doing those things based on their importance, can be the difference between bumbling through life and having control of your life.

Thinking about and using lists as suggested should increase your productivity and reduce your stress.

QUESTIONS

1. Do you use lists to help you remember all of the things you need to do? If not, why not? Would you consider using lists?

2. If you do use lists, what are the differences between how you use lists and how the chapter suggests lists should be used?

3. When you used lists in the past, did you find that they gave you some degree of stress because you thought of them as needing to be completed each day? What can you do to change this?

4. Can you think of anyone or any occupation that would not need to use lists at least some of the time?

5. Which makes more sense to you: to make your list and prioritize it at the end of the day or to make your list and prioritize it first thing in the morning? What are the reasons for your choice?

ACTIVITIES

1. Define *prioritization* and give examples. Share your definitions in the group.

2. What are some high priorities among people your age? Base your answer on behavior that you have observed. Do you agree that these should be high priorities? What high priorities do you think people your age should have? Discuss the answers among the members of the group. Do answers vary? Does this activity have any relationship to your daily list?

3. Interview some people you judge to be successful. Ask them if they use lists and how they use those lists. Share this information with members of the group. Make a master list of how lists are used by successful people. Compare that list to the suggestions made in this chapter. Should anything be added, deleted, or modified?

4. Try using a list for at least one week. Use the list to remember what you need to do. Prioritize the list and do the things that are most important. Construct your list for the next day the night before. Carry over the incomplete tasks to the next day. Congratulate yourself for what you have accomplished. Be proud that what you completed was high priority while what you did not complete was low priority. Keep brief notes of how this experiment works and report to the group. Share your experiences and your evaluation of this approach to

goals. How would you modify this approach to make it better?

CHAPTER 7

Choose to Be Better, Not Perfect

The ideas we have about life make a big difference in how successful and happy we can be. An excellent example of this is the difference in thinking between a person who is a perfectionist and a person who is a realist. Which one of these ways of thinking is most like yours?

The Perfectionist

The perfectionist thinks, "I won't be happy until I'm perfect." The perfectionist won't be happy:

- Unless his hair is just perfect (no matter what I do, my hair is never right).

- Until her figure is just perfect (I am so far from having the figure I want, why even try to change?)

- Until his teeth are perfectly straight (I'm doomed to look ugly with these teeth. They will never look right, no matter what I do to them or how much money I spend).

- Until her complexion is flawless (I just know that I'm going to get a zit before the party and I'll just die!)

Perfectionistic parents expect their little children to be perfect even when they are in a store full of interesting things to explore. If the child "misbehaves" (e.g., picks up an interesting but breakable object like a colorful glass vase), the parent is unhappy with the child and with himself for not being a perfect parent. Because the parent thinks in perfectionist terms and expects the child to behave like an angel, there are two unhappy people.

Another example of the true perfectionist is the person who wants to have perfect grades all through school. When she finally gets a grade of "B," it devastates her. Instead of being happy about her excellent academic record, she is unhappy because of one little deviation from perfection. Isn't it amazing how our thinking influences our happiness?

You can probably think of other examples of people who have set unrealistic goals of perfection for themselves or others or who couldn't meet their impossible standards and finally gave up trying. Perhaps you can even think of some personal examples. Instead of changing their habits of thinking in perfectionist standards, they stopped trying altogether. The perfectionist needs to realize that nobody is perfect, but everybody can get better.

It's Better to Get Better

A more realistic way to think about life is to strive for improvement rather than perfection. The realist thinks, "I don't expect to be perfect, but I can get better—and each time I get better, I will feel successful and be happier."

The realist is happy when:

- She loses two inches off her hips (It really feels good to know that I have control over my body and can make myself look and feel better).

- He starts a savings plan, even if it is only $25.00 a month (I know it isn't much to save by some people's standards, but it is a great start for me).

- She smokes fewer cigarettes now as she works toward quitting completely (I am smoking less now, and I am proud of my accomplishment even though it might take a while longer for me to quit completely).

- He deliberately thinks positive thoughts more than he did when he was a negative thinker (I still think negative thoughts sometimes, but now I catch myself and look for the positive in the person or the situation).

If you want to change yourself or the situation, you should strive to set goals of improvement rather than trying to attain goals of perfection. Even if you were able to attain perfection, it isn't likely that you could maintain the 100 percent perfection for very long. Even "experts" make mistakes. You and I shouldn't allow ourselves to think in these 100 percent terms but should instead think about improvement.

One of the main advantages of thinking in terms of getting better is that it is easier to get better than it is to get perfect, let alone stay perfect. I can be quite happy with my improvement as a tennis player from month to month, but I would be very frustrated if I wanted to be perfect. Each time I am happy with myself for my improvement, I gain confidence in myself and am more likely to make further gains. This "success leads to more success" is well known in all walks of life, but in athletics is known as "momentum." In fact, you might want to define success as any improvement in your life or any progress toward your goals, no matter how small. This way of thinking

65

could make a big difference in how successful and happy you feel.

Another valuable aspect of seeking improvement rather than perfection is that thinking about improvement always keeps you thinking in the positive. Your thinking about having to be perfect is based on the negative idea that you are inadequate unless you make no mistakes. You are striving for the impossible and are likely to be thinking about the large distance between you and the state of perfection you desire. You are also thinking about how much work you still have to do or about how much there still is to be accomplished because perfection, by its nature, is always a long way off in the distance. In contrast, if you are a person who is realistically trying to get better, you will be looking for the small, positive gains you make and take satisfaction in each improvement. You will be thinking about how successful you are now instead of how successful you will be someday when you are perfect.

The next time you decide there is something in your life that you want to change, you should consider the strategy of becoming better, not perfect. You need long-term goals, but don't let them be your only criteria for success. Be more realistic by breaking down long-term goals into small, attainable increments of improvement, which become your measures of success. Get into the habit of seeking, identifying, and rewarding yourself for small increments of progress. Develop the habit of celebrating each of these successes and taking pride in each small accomplishment rather than taking your achievements for granted and thinking about how much there is left to do.

The concept of exchanging the impossibility of "being perfect" for realistically "getting better" is another example of how our lives are determined by the ways we think and the habits we develop. You and you alone possess the power to change your thinking and your habits to make your life more productive, more successful, and happier.

This is a fantastic power—if you use it.

QUESTIONS

1. In what ways are you a perfectionist? Do you set unrealistic standards of perfection for yourself? Other people? Animals? Your work? Your looks? Cleanliness? Children?

2. What kind of relationship can you make between being a perfectionist and being happy? Use an example of people about your own age.

3. It has been observed that perfectionists often do not try new, adventurous things. Why do you suppose that happens? Has it ever happened to you?

ACTIVITIES

1. Look up the word *perfect* in the dictionary. Considering the definitions for the word, do you think anyone can be perfect? In what part of life could a person possibly be perfect? Even if one could attain perfection, do you think he or she could maintain it for any length of time?

2. Do you agree with the quote, "A perfectionist is doomed to be unhappy most of the time"? Why or why not? What do others in your group think? If you don't agree with the quote, how would you change it so that you could agree with it?

3. Can you show a major idea about "getting better instead of trying to be perfect" using a chart, cartoon, drawing, or other visual medium? This won't be easy, but give it a try. Share your creation with others in your group. See if they understand your illustrated idea without you having to explain it to them.

4. Explain how the idea of improvement and the idea that success breeds success are related. Use some original examples.

5. List at least five examples of statements someone might make that indicate he or she is a perfectionist. Have others in your group share their statements. Listen carefully so that you can give appropriate feedback to

others. Also, make modifications in your examples based on others' feedback to your statements.

CHAPTER 8
Decision-Making and Human Consequences

We live at a time in history when change is taking place at an ever-increasing rate. Previously accepted traditions, mores, ideals, and practices are being questioned as never before. The status quo rug is being pulled, if not jerked, from under us.

Institutions and individuals now have the opportunity to make decisions in areas that previously were not open to alternatives. In the "good old days," most of the decisions were made by those in authority. Areas in our lives such as politics, religion, education, vocations, and human relationships now contain more options and alternatives than ever from which we can choose. Over the years, most of us have gained more control over decisions that affect our lives. We have also become more aware that we always have choices, regardless of the situation, and that how we decide is extremely important to our lives and happiness.

There is now much written about how to make decisions. There are many skills, techniques, and procedures that you can use; however, there is much less written about how you can judge the value of your decisions. What constitutes a good decision? How do you know when one decision is better than another one?

The premise on which this chapter is built is that better decisions will be made if they are focused on consequences—human consequences—as best as they can be determined. That is, one criterion that can be, and should be, applied to any decision is, "What will happen to people if this decision is acted upon?" This does not mean that human consequences are the only criterion by which to judge the worth of a decision; however, it would seem unwise to act on a hypothesis without first contemplating the probable consequences to human beings. *In short, the greater the positive human consequences, the more confident you can be that the decision is a good one.*

The concept of human consequences as the basis of decision making can be facilitated by the use of a four-part matrix. One axis contains *Consequences for Self* and *Consequences for Others.* The other axis contains *Short-Term Consequences* and *Long-Term Consequences.* Each of the quadrants is used to record the predicted positive and negative consequences arising from the decision. These predictions can be given different values by the participants if some seem to be more important than others. For example, when buying a car you might give higher values to economy and safety than you would to speed. One person or an entire group can use the strategy. The strategy can be applied to individual decisions or can be used for decisions that could influence large masses of people, such as those made by the government.

A form such as the following could be used.

HUMAN CONSEQUENCES MATRIX

Decision to be acted upon

	SHORT-TERM		LONG-TERM	
	POSITIVE	NEGATIVE	POSITIVE	NEGATIVE
CONSEQUENSES FOR SELF				
CONSEQUENSES FOR OTHERS	POSITIVE NEGATIVE		POSITIVE NEGATIVE	

☐ I should act on this decision.
☐ I should not act on this decision.
☐ I cannot decide at this time (need more information, time, etc.)

Your use of a matrix such as the one above will not guarantee that your decisions will be good ones; however, the consideration of the consequences of a given decision in terms of oneself and others in the near and distant future should increase the probability that gross harm to human beings will be avoided. How many decisions in the past could have been made desirable if human consequences had been a priority? How many decisions will be made by governments, teachers, parents, business people, and you and me with a deliberate consideration of what happens to people as the major criterion? **How many future decisions can we afford to make without deliberately and predominantly considering their human consequences?**

You might want to add other types of consequences in some cases. For example, city officials might want to consider "consequences for the environment" when making decisions about roads, parks, or zoning. Perhaps that particular consequence should always be on all the matrices.

It is on mine.

QUESTIONS

1. From your understanding of history, do you think that people today have more choices to make than those who lived before us? Think about areas such as vocations, things to purchase, travel, and so on. Give examples to support your answers. Perhaps you can interview older people for perspective.

2. Do you agree with the idea that "the best decisions are those that have the most positive human consequences and the poorest decisions are those that have the most negative human consequences"? Explain your answer. Use examples.

3. If you disagree that "what happens to human beings is one of the most important ways to judge the value of a decision," what would you use to judge how valuable a decision is? Give an example or two as you explain your answer.

4. Explain in your own words what is meant by "predictions recorded in the matrix can be 'weighted' by the participants if some seem more important than others." Be sure to use original examples.

5. In which of the four quadrants would you find the most "immature" behavior represented? Explain.

6. Which of the four quadrants do you think would be the most difficult to predict? Which would be the next most difficult to predict? Explain your answers and use original examples.

7. Which of the four quadrants do you think would represent the most "selfish" behavior? Explain.

8. If you were a news reporter interviewing a government official about his position on a bill, how could you use the matrix to develop questions to ask?

ACTIVITIES

1. Describe in writing how you usually make a decision. What are the ways that you normally judge whether your decision is a good one or not? For example, some people list all the positive aspects in one column, all the negative aspects in another column, and then decide based on which list is the longest. Describing your usual decision-making process will probably be a difficult task because we don't often take the time to analyze how we make decisions. If you can't identify a general pattern to your decision-making, think of a recent decision you made and analyze the process you used. How does your process differ from the human consequences one described in this chapter?

2. Do you have a real decision that you will be making in the near future? Perhaps it is a decision that you have been putting off for a while. Using the matrix in this chapter, apply the human consequences approach to your decision. Does the matrix help? Would you add anything to the matrix to help others arrive at a better decision?

3. Real decisions are the best to use, but if you can't think of one, you might use one of the following to practice using the human consequences matrix. Pretend that you are:

- A junior in high school who is thinking about dropping out of school

- A 15-year-old girl who is thinking about running away from home

- A husband and wife who are thinking about having their first child

- A boy who is a sophomore in college and a girl who is a senior in high school thinking about getting married in four months

- A person who is thinking about purchasing a car and can't decide between a used one that will cost less and a new one that will cost much more

4. When you have practiced the human consequences matrix for a time or two, do you have any problems with its application? Is there anything that is especially difficult? Is there anything that you would change? Discuss these questions in your group. Would your group modify the matrix in any way? If so, present your modifications and your reasons.

5. Think of a decision that you made some time ago that has already had some human consequences. Apply the human consequences matrix to what you know has happened to you and others in the short-term and the long-term as a result of your making that decision. Based on this analysis, would you say the decision was a good one? This is a way that you can judge any part of history, whether it is yours, a president's, or a country's.

6. You might find it interesting to apply the human consequences matrix to a person who made a famous decision in history. One of the most famous decisions occurred when President Harry Truman decided to drop

atomic bombs on Nagasaki and Hiroshima, Japan, in World War II. Based on human consequences, was it a good decision? What information did he know when he made the decision? What different information would have helped him to make a better decision? If you were President Truman in World War II, would you have dropped atomic bombs on these two cities knowing what you know now?

7. Can you create a situation in which a person using the human consequences matrix would justifiably say that a decision could not be reached? Explain.

CHAPTER 9

The World Is Not Fair

Some people live long and happy lives while others die very young. Some people are born to rich families and others are born into poverty. Some people are attractive by the prevailing standards and others appear unattractive. Innocent children are killed. The nicest lady in town gets an incurable disease. The obviously guilty criminal goes free. A drunken driver causes an accident that kills a whole family, but the drunk isn't even scratched. The world is not fair.

What can you do when something unfair happens to you?

Accept the fact that life is not fair. You are not the first person who had something unjust happen to her or him. You will not be the last. Bad things happen to good people and good things happen to bad people. Being a good person will not protect you from unfair happenings in your life any more than being a vegetarian would protect you from being eaten by a starving lion. This is not to discourage you from being the best person you can be. It is simply pointing out that no matter how considerate, thoughtful, and wonderful a person you might be as

81

a teenager, you still might get a big pimple on your nose the day of your most important date. Life isn't fair. In fact, it might be good mental health practice not to think of events as being "fair" or "unfair." Just think of them simply as events or as the environment giving you feedback. Then it is less tempting to dwell on "your unfair treatment."

Don't dwell on it. The most important thing to remember when something unfair happens to you is not to dwell on it. Put it behind you where it belongs. Forget it as best you can. Whatever has happened, no matter how unjust you think it is, it's in the past. There is nothing you can do about what has already happened. Far too many people spend their lives bemoaning past events. Young widows have spent substantial parts of the rest of their lives trying to answer questions like, "Why did this happen to me?" A scarred survivor of a freak accident is immobilized by constantly thinking about how unfair his situation is. When you dwell on a past event, you are simply using up your present life thinking about what you didn't want to have happen to you in your past life. This is a terrible waste of your precious present life.

Emphasize what you DO have. When something unfair happens to you, emphasize what you have rather than what you have lost. This is closely related to the idea that you should not dwell on the unfair event. For example, if you were a person who had lost a leg in an accident that was not your fault, you would want as quickly as possible to plan how best to use the strengths you have left rather than to depress yourself by thinking about how you have been lessened. You would still have your mind, the rest of your body, your personality, friends, and a whole host of other qualities on which you could build. While it is probably true that of the 10,000 things you could do with both legs you can now only do 8,500, you need to become

82

involved in those things you *can* do. Thinking must shift from bemoaning the loss of the 1,500 things you could do prior to the accident to the 8,500 opportunities you still have available to you. This crucial shift in thinking is necessary if you are to overcome the accident. Much of mental health and happiness is based on this idea of appreciating and using what you have rather than lamenting what you do not have. It is especially crucial when you are dealing with a situation that could be considered unfair or unjust in some way. Accentuate the positive in your life. They are your building blocks. You can't build your life on negatives or on the opportunities that have been taken away by an unfair world. Successful and happy people never dwell, at least not for long, on their liabilities. Such people are too busy building with their assets.

Sooner or later, something will happen to you that you will perceive to be unfair. It's almost a guarantee. Of course, the world doesn't know that it is being unfair and doesn't really care. In reality, the issue of "fairness" is really unimportant, and you shouldn't waste your time on it. The best approach is simply to count the blessings you have left and go on with your wonderful miracle of life from there.

And when you have the feeling that life is being somehow unfair to you, think about how fair is it that out of all the uncountable possibilities.

You were given the fantastic opportunity of life.

QUESTIONS

1. What is meant by the word "fair" when it refers to relationships among people or between people and the environment? In other words, how do you define fairness?

2. Why does the author suggest that you should accept the fact that the world is not fair?

3. Using your definition of fair, do you think the world is fair?

4. Do you think the world could be or should be fair?

5. What could you specifically do to make the world more "fair"?

6. If you can't make the world completely fair, how can you deal with it?

ACTIVITIES

1. Make a list of all the ways you can think of that people
    have tried to make the world fairer. For example, people in
    governments make laws that they believe will make their
    community fairer.

2. Imagine a situation where you accidentally lost one of your
    senses or one of your limbs. Then list the things that you
    would not be able to do after the accident that you could
    do before the accident. What would you still be able to do?
    Describe how you could utilize what you still can do and
    how you would have to accept what you can't do. Contrast
    this behavior with what would happen if you spent your
    time being unhappy with what you had lost.

3. Describe a real or hypothetical problem where a dilemma
    arises because people have different ideas of fairness. For
    example, two sisters are hungry and find two apples in
    their refrigerator. One of the apples is considerably larger.
    The older sister thinks it is fair if she gets that apple
    because she is older. The younger sister thinks that it
    would be fair if they flipped a coin and the winner would
    get the bigger apple. The sisters' mother thinks it would
    be fair if the older daughter would allow the younger
    daughter to have the bigger apple. Which do you believe
    is fair? Why? How would you solve this problem to make
    it fair?

CHAPTER 10

Making Successful Changes in Your Life

You probably wouldn't be reading this if you weren't already thinking about changing something in your life. What specific changes would you like to have happen? You will find it most helpful if you take the time right now to write down your most important change and apply to it the ideas presented so far in this book. No! Don't read on. Write down your desired change now before you proceed.

Some Major Considerations

You cannot progress without change, but you can change without progress. You have to participate in some kind of change if you are going to get better at something or improve some part of your life. It does not matter if you want to be a better student, sibling, parent, tennis player, teacher, spouse, reader, driver, or anything else; you have to change some aspect of your life. This involves areas of your life, such as habits, knowledge, skills, time allocations, mindsets, expectations, self-esteem, and confidence, among others. You must determine to what extent the change you have chosen represents progress. Be careful not to equate change with progress. A poorly-chosen change can result in everything from wasted time to severely negative consequences to yourself and others.

A change should move you toward the positive. When you visualize your change, do you see yourself going toward a positive improvement or do you see yourself escaping from a negative thing? Sometimes you want to change simply to get away from something, and you accomplish it only to find that you are in an even worse situation. This situation is represented by the saying "out of the frying pan and into the fire." For example, some kids run away from home without planning what they will do when they "escape." Almost always, they find that the world outside home is much more undesirable than what they were experiencing at home. Perhaps change should be treated as most people treat moving to a different house or apartment. We move to lodgings that will be better for us in terms of comfort, cost, attractiveness, or convenience. We usually have a positive reason for our move. You should always think in positive terms when making a change in your life. Go toward what you desire—not just away from what you find undesirable.

A change should be planned in specific terms. Your thinking and goals should be specific. You don't want to think in general terms like, "I want to be happier," when you should be thinking something like, "Every time I catch myself feeling sorry for myself or thinking negatively, I am going to stop and find the positives in the situation."

Most changes should be thought of as lifestyle changes. If you are going to make changes in your life, make a change that you will continue the rest of your life. Millions of people go on diets in attempts to lose weight quickly and painlessly. Even if they achieve their weight loss goals, they almost always go off the diet and return to their old habits and to their original overweight condition. If you desire to lose weight, you would want to change your way of living (your lifestyle) so that you could reach your desired weight and then maintain it. This means making changes in your nutrition and exercise lifestyle that you can live with for the rest of your life.

It's better to have a small change than to have no change at all. Here is an all-too-often repeated situation at my fitness club. A new and motivated member of the club, despite many warnings, works out too long and with too much intensity for the first few visits. He or she gets sore, doesn't like the pain, and does not come back. Rather than make some progress, the new member overdid it and ended up quitting with no progress. Long-lasting changes are built on realistic, smaller incremental steps rather than sudden, all-or-nothing approaches. Your change is more likely to be achieved if you break it down into these realistic incremental steps. For example, most wealthy people have saved small amounts of money periodically and consistently over a long period of time. Playing the lottery is hoping that you can become wealthy by luck when your odds are millions to one. These smaller steps are not only easier to achieve, but they also provide more successes to keep you motivated.

Change to get better—not perfect. It's okay to pursue perfection, but don't feel that you have to be perfect. This idea is closely related to the idea that some progress is better than no progress. Perfection is something that you and I can have as an ideal goal to keep us headed in a general direction, but it is not realistic to think that we can become perfect people who don't make mistakes and never will. It is this kind of thinking that leads us to abandon a change because we can't reach our own self-imposed and unrealistic standards of perfection. We doom ourselves from the start. You might best think of yourself as someone in control of your life who can improve when you want to, but who is too smart to get caught in the perfection trap.

Don't get upset by the temporary slowing of your progress now and then. While you are making your change, unfortunate events are going to happen from time to time. For example, you have recently begun saving some money each month, but you may have an unforeseen expense that will not allow you to put any money in your savings that month. This is disappointing, but it isn't a catastrophe. You should accept it as an unfortunate event, feel good about how much you have already been able to save, and continue your monthly savings as soon as you can. Learn to treat these "setbacks" as temporary and controllable inconveniences.

Treat change as an adventure. Some people interpret changes in their lives as being stressful. Every change has the potential of being stressful because there is always the factor of risk and the unknown about it. Something new and unexpected might occur, and you cannot be sure if it will be positive or negative. It is interesting that these same qualities of risk, the unknown, the unexpected, and the new that are associated with stress are also the qualities that describe a good adventure. You can make your change into an exciting, adventurous life experience or you can make it into a stressful struggle. It depends on how you think about it and what you expect.

You seldom change one thing. This is what economists refer to as "externalities" or unintended consequences. Some people call this the "ripple effect." It happens when we make a change but other changes also happen that we did not intend. For example, you decide that you will ride a bicycle to work to save money. You do save money and are happy about that; however, you find that there are also consequences you didn't anticipate such as harsh weather causing you to arrive at work dirty, soaking wet, or late. There could also be positive consequences you didn't think about such as being more physically fit and losing weight. Try to anticipate all the consequences of the change you want to work. Maybe someone else could help you see consequences you might not think of and give needed perspective to your desired change.

Four Factors Necessary for Change

Any change you undertake is going to have to satisfy at least four criteria if that change is going to be implemented and sustained. To have a successful change, you will need to have the desire to change, the knowledge to change, the effort expended to change, and the right environment to allow the change. Again, analyze your proposed change to see if these four factors are satisfied.

The desire to change. The desire to change starts with a dissatisfaction of the status quo. In some way, you visualize that your life can be better. At this point, most people make one of two choices. First, you can visualize a better life but only gripe and complain about how unlucky and miserable you are, then do nothing about it; or, second, you might visualize a better life, maybe complain a little bit, but spend most of your time figuring out what you can do about it. You know that you are in control of your life, and if you want it to be better you will have to make some changes.

The intensity of your desire to change is directly proportional to the amount of effort you will expend in getting the knowledge to bring about the change and implementing the change over a long period of time. This is crucial to you, but it is also crucial for anyone else who is going to help you to partner in your change. Will they have the same amount of drive as you do? For example, if you were going to open a new business and had two partners in mind, it would be very important to know the degree of desire they had to see the business succeed. Desire for a change is closely associated with the commitment to it. This is why you want to be very sure that the changes you undertake are really important to you and are among your highest priorities.

The knowledge to change. Many attempts to change something have failed because those implementing the change did not have the knowledge to make it a success. Have you ever had the experience of being excited about doing something and just started doing it without knowing what you were doing? What usually happens in a case like this is that the highly motivated person uses inappropriate skills and knowledge, and the change doesn't progress as he or she had anticipated. That person becomes less motivated, expends less effort, and gets even more negative results until he or she eventually gives up. This is common with people who desire to change their nutrition and exercise lifestyles. They really want to be healthier, look better, and feel better, but they don't take the time to find out how to accomplish these changes. They confuse activity with progress. The result is often no change, a feeling of defeat, frustration, and a loss of self-esteem. Many new businesses are started by enthusiastic entrepreneurs who eventually fail because they didn't take the time to learn the business. *If your change is worth doing, it is worth the time and effort to research how best to do it.* This research and planning stage often takes more time than the actual implementation of the change, so be patient.

The effort to change. No matter how much desire you have and how much knowledge you have, no change will be successful unless you expend the effort to bring it about. You can desperately want to be wealthy, and you can have the appropriate knowledge and skills needed to become wealthy, but it won't happen until you stop procrastinating and actually take action. Many great change *plans* are never acted upon because the change *agent* is too busy entertaining himself.

The environment must allow the change. This necessary factor includes all the aspects of the environment in which your change is to be implemented. As someone who wants to bring about a change, you will need to be a student of the environment around you. You need to analyze the environment for any part of it that might hinder or block your change. For example, you might want to be wealthier, have the knowledge of how to become wealthier, and be willing to expend the effort, but upon checking the environment, find that it is illegal. Many people find that their new lifestyles in smoking, nutrition, exercise, and finance are often hindered or blocked by members of their family or group of friends. Some other parts of the environment that can work against change are our limitations (both real and often imagined) of money, time, education, skills, location, and others. *You will probably find that the biggest and most permanent obstacles are those manufactured between your ears.*

A quick method of formally identifying the parts of the environment that are working for and against your change is called "force field analysis." Make a list of all the things you can think of that are factors that promote your change. Then make a list of all the things that are factors that hinder your change. Now you can better determine the probable success of your change. You may find that there are hindering forces so strong that you will have to postpone your change until you can remove or transform the hindering factor.

In summary, it is important to note that change is one of the most permanent things in your life. Change will always be a part of your future. Change imparts variety to your life. Change allows you to improve your life. Change can add adventure to your life. You can simply let the changes happen and hope for the best, or you can use your power to initiate and control much of that change.

It's your choice.

QUESTIONS

1. Do you agree with the statement, "You cannot progress without change, but you can change without progress"? Support your answer with examples.

2. What is the risk in just making a change to avoid an unpleasant or undesirable situation rather than making a change to move toward a positive or desired situation?

3. Do you believe that "it is better to have a small change than to have no change at all"? Why or why not? How does this idea relate to the idea of breaking down a big change into many small changes?

4. Do you believe that one of the four factors for change (desire, knowledge, effort, and environment) is more important than the other three? If so, explain. Are any of the four factors for change less important? Is it less important to the extent that it isn't even needed?

5. How do you describe in your own words the statement found in the discussion on the environment needed for change: "You will probably find that the biggest and most permanent obstacles are those manufactured between your ears"? Do you think this statement might be true in parts of your life other than when you're trying to make a change? Explain and give examples.

ACTIVITIES

1. Imagine that you decide you want to change to a healthier lifestyle. You say that the goal of your change is to "be in better physical condition." What specific steps would you suggest you take to make your goal clearer and to begin the necessary activities? Share the specifics of this change with your group. Discuss what will be the best specific plan by putting all the ideas together.

2. What does the idea, "Change to get better, not to be perfect," have to do with sustaining a change that you have created? Use examples. Share with the group and modify your answers to get better feedback from the members.

3. Think of a situation where you want to have someone else change in a way that you believe would make his or her life better. If possible, think of a real person and a real change. For example, you would like to change a member of your family by having him or her cut down on or quit smoking cigarettes. Apply the four factors necessary for sustaining change to your efforts to help your relative change. What strategies would you use in applying those factors? Share your strategies with others in the group and have them give you feedback on your applications of the factors.

4. Stress can accompany change because changes always involve some degree of the unknown. One way to take some of the possible stress out of change is to think of the change as an adventure. Can you explain how thinking of change as an adventure would reduce the apprehension and fear that

almost always accompanies it? What other ways can you visualize to reduce the fear of the unknown? Make a master list of these ways of reducing the probability of stress by using the input of all the members of your group.

5. Imagine that you want to change your lifestyle to one that is very simple and healthy. One of the things that you want to change is that the only liquid you will drink is pure water. You will drink no other beverages of any kind. You have the desire and the knowledge, and you're willing to expend the effort. Now, analyze to what extent your environment will allow you to make your change by using the simplified version of "force field analysis" mentioned in the chapter to see which factors promote your change and which factors hinder your change. What did you discover? Who else might be appropriate to help you complete this task?

6. Compare the Nike shoe company slogan, "Just do it," with the second factor for change: gaining the knowledge of how to change. Are these consistent with each other? Support your answer with examples. If you think they are not compatible, how would you change the slogan to make it consistent with the idea of gaining knowledge?

7. What is the most important change that you anticipate making in the near future? Apply the four criteria necessary for sustained voluntary change to your change. What did you discover about the change? Will you need more information or do you think you can begin the change immediately? Will

you need to change something in the environment before beginning the change process?

8. Make a poster, chart, or other visual display showing the four factors of change.

9. Can you think of any factors necessary for change that should be added to the list of four that are in this chapter? Explain and illustrate your addition if you have one or more.

CHAPTER 11

Live in the Moment Without Sacrificing the Future for Yourself or Others

Live in the moment. This simple idea is one of the keys to living a fuller and happier life. Perhaps it is the key to a life of more enjoyment and a greater number of peak experiences. It focuses your attention on the present moment in your life. For example, how are you experiencing this particular moment in your life? Do you feel good? Are you mentally alert? Are you getting involved in the idea of "living in the moment" and already beginning to apply it to yourself? How aware are you of the sights, sounds, textures, smells, or tastes at this moment? Think about it. This moment is your life.

You have yourself and this moment. Your past is time that you have already used up and is simply gone and your future is potential time that might be available but is not guaranteed to you. The only time that you really have is the present time. You should make the most of it. The following are ideas about living in the present. Some of them will be ideas that you can use to make your life a more productive and enjoyable one.

Find enjoyment in the common things in your life.
Think about enjoying the cold drink of water, the warm cup of tea, the smile on a person's face, the feeling of the cool breeze on a warm day, the joy of a good laugh, the aroma of a perfume or flower, the feel of soft cloth, the taste of the food you eat, or watching a child completely enthralled in play. We take the usual things in our life for granted. Take a new look at the things you do as part of your daily rituals and discover how you can deliberately find the most enjoyment in them. For example, you might have to drive a long distance to and from work in heavy traffic. You might find it stressful and boring. What could you do to make this time more interesting and valuable? The simple things in life can be the most enjoyable things in life.

Choose the everyday things in your life for the happiness they will bring you. This is the reverse of the first idea, which encourages you to find enjoyment in the things you already do. This idea is to choose the things you do for their potential of being enjoyable.

The most obvious choice for many people would be their jobs. If you could choose a job that you really love to do, you would not find it to be "work." It would be an activity that would make more of your working hours a series of enjoyable moments. Many people choose their vocations on the basis of how much money they will make and then discover that their jobs are not enjoyable or fulfilling. If you find your job can be unhappy and unfulfilled part of your life, perhaps you should consider changing to a different job in which you could find more fulfillment and enjoyment. These ideal jobs are usually ones in which you are involved in creatively using your special interests and skills doing something you consider worthwhile. This "doing" can be the production of something valuable or the delivery of some kind of useful service. What special interests or talents do you have that you would love to pursue in more depth? Does your present position encourage creative use of your talents and interests? If so, great! If not, what is keeping you from choosing to pursue these interests further as the basis for a vocation?

If your special interests and skills cannot be pursued as a job, perhaps you could pursue them as a hobby or second vocation. The creative uses of your interests and skills are possibilities for an ideal avocation. Think of those times when you become completely and enjoyably engrossed in doing a hobby you love. These times are perfect examples of living in the moment, and you might want to set aside more time for these peak experiences if you can think of some way to make them your "regular job." For example, you might love to make pottery but can't make a living doing it. So keep your regular job to make money and make pottery in your spare time.

Many of the happiest and most successful people have made choices in their lives whereby their vocations and avocations are the same. That is, they consider their jobs to be their hobbies. They make their livelihoods doing their hobbies. That's an interesting concept that you might want to pursue.

No one is completely happy all the time. Do not interpret any part of this chapter to mean that you must be continually ecstatic or you're some kind of failure. Like most things in life, happiness is a matter of degree. You want to get the most enjoyment possible in the present moment, but you do not want to set the unrealistic goal of being completely happy all the time. If you set your goals too high, you can add to your stress rather than to your happiness. You can become happier but you can never be *completely* happy, at least not for very long.

Enjoy what you have now. Too many people think about what they don't have and don't enjoy what they have now. They are like the person who has $100 and somehow loses $1. He can then think about the money he lost but be happy that he still has the $99. In the same way, you can choose to use your present moment's appreciation of being "rich" with what you have, or you can spend the moment feeling like a "loser." There are other people who think about how happy they will be when they get something in the future but don't enjoy what they have right then. They are like the person who has $100 but won't be happy until they get $200. They choose not to spend their present moment being happy with $100. Instead, they choose to be presently *un*happy until they have twice the amount of money. Note that they could be quite happy with their present money and still make plans to work for more. The problem occurs when we continually use up our present moment thinking about the past or the future.

The reality is that you won't always be able to be focused on the present. It's not easy to draw yourself into the present moment if you are not in the habit of doing so. One set of strategies you might use is to become deliberately aware of your immediate surroundings. This awareness can help you focus on the present moment. Reach out and touch different things around you. Feel the textures. Look around you and notice the colors, patterns, shapes, and so on. What do you smell, what sounds do you hear, and are you tasting anything? This is how you can use one or more of your senses to draw yourself into the present. That is, when you become aware that your mind has drifted out of the present, you might focus on the present sounds for a moment to bring you back into the present moment. Of course, you could use any of your senses. Another means of becoming more aware of your present is thinking of a spot in the middle of your forehead or becoming aware of different parts of your own body. You might want to adopt one of these devices to get centered in the present moment when you catch yourself spending too much time thinking about the past or the future.

Deliberately living in the present moment carries with it an obligation to others. It is immoral for you to live in the moment if it is done at the cost of harming others. For example, it is immoral for one generation to deliberately use up irreplaceable natural resources or to irreparably pollute the environment for generations to come. Living in the present moment carries with it the obligation to respect the rights of others to enjoy their own present moments. Living in the moment is never being selfish at the expense of others. Living in the moment always includes acting responsibly toward the environment, others, and yourself.

Living in the moment does not exclude planning for the future. It is foolish and shortsighted to live only in the present moment. You must plan for the future and try to influence the future to be as ideal as possible. You never want to live in the present moment at the expense of your future. Extreme examples of this occur when people alter their minds with drugs to get abnormal sensations for short periods of time without regard for the long-term consequences. These are attempts to get quick and easy enjoyment in the present moment without regard for the well-known future complications of addiction, criminality, permanent mind alterations, and even death. Living in the moment without due regard for your future is a good example of immature, if not immoral, behavior.

When you make a decision, enjoy the results of the decision. Do not second-guess your decision. If you decide to have a snake as your pet, enjoy the snake and don't think about whether a dog or a cat might have been more fun.

If you want to observe living in the moment at its best, watch children as they play or creative people as they create. The young child can become captivated with the play. There is no thought about the past or the future, and there is no concern about what others might be thinking or saying. There is total concentration on whatever is happening at the moment. The same thing is true of the person who gives no thought to problems while in the act of creating something. There is total involvement, excitement, and enjoyment in the task of the moment. These peak experiences can be mental and physical "highs" that are far better, safer, and more productive than those that are drug-induced.

You might try using guided imagery to increase your enjoyment of the moment. Try affirmations such as, "I always look for enjoyment in whatever I do," or, "I am finding more and more peak experiences in my life every day," or, "I frequently stop myself and determine how I can enjoy that very moment." Make signs like these and put them where you can see them every day.

A major key to enjoying the moment is always looking for the positive side of the immediate situation. When you're happy, you're in some way having a good time. If you get in the habit of looking for the good in any situation, you're more likely to find it. In any given moment, you can be focused on what is enjoyable in the situation or you can focus on what can make you unhappy. Looking for the positive is the *outlook* on life that can *change* your life. If you also focus on the present moment, you're looking for the "positive present." This has two meanings. You can have a positive present, which can mean an "enjoyable present moment." You can also have a positive present, which means a "positive gift" that you can give to yourself and others by focusing your thoughts on the positives of the moment.

This seems so simple. You would expect we would all make it a first-tier habit. Will you?

QUESTIONS

1. Would you explain the idea "live in the moment without sacrificing the future for yourself or others" to a person who had never heard of the idea? Give clear examples.

2. What are things you could do to help yourself focus on the present moment? For example, become aware of the sounds of the moment.

3. Are there times when you should not want to focus on the present moment? When? Why?

4. What are some cautions we should consider when we are focusing on the present moment in our lives?

5. Explain how "second-guessing" your decisions can keep you from being as happy as you can be. Use an original example or two.

6. As explained in the chapter, little children at play are one of the best examples of living in the moment. Why do you think that we could concentrate so intensely on the moment when we were children, but as we grew older this became more difficult?

ACTIVITIES

1. Using the words *past, present* and *future*, explain the idea of "living in the moment."

2. Make a list of the common things that give you enjoyment (for example, a cold drink of water on a very hot day). Have others in the group share theirs. Did you get any new ideas of ways to enjoy the everyday things of life? Did you find differences in defining common things in your life?

3. Write ways in which you could focus on a common thing you do every day so that it brings enjoyment to you (for example, brushing your teeth, choosing your clothes for that day, or combing your hair).

4. Interview people about the jobs they have. What are the best things about their work? What would they like to change about their work? Do they often become so engrossed or interested in their jobs that they lose track of the rest of the world around them? Would you say that any of the people you interviewed have a vocation they love?

5. Would you rather have Job A that is a position you love and pays a modern living wage or Job B that is a position you dislike but pays a wage twice as much as Job A? What are your reasons? Have others in the group share

their answers and reasons. How many chose Job A? How many chose Job B?

6. Pretend that you and some friends are shipwrecked on an island and that you will never be found; however, a magic genie appears and says she will supply you with food, water, shelter, and any other necessities of life. In addition, you can have your choice of 10 things for you to enjoy for the rest of your life. These things will last forever and/or will be replenished, but you will get nothing else for the rest of your life. You need to be very careful what you choose. Make a list of those 10 things and share the answers among your group. After everyone has shared, take some time to modify your list if you think that it is warranted. Then share what your changes were and why you made them.

7. Make a list of things that a person could do to enjoy the present moment that would sacrifice the future for that person. Make a list of things that a person could do to enjoy the present moment but that could sacrifice the future of other people. How many of the items on the two lists are the same? How many could involve people your age?

8. Many people say that they find it easier to live in the moment when they use their talents doing something creative and interesting. Does this fit you? Explain.

9. The following is a list of situations. You and a partner are to choose a situation cooperatively. Now flip a coin. "Heads" writes how a person could look at the situation in a positive way, and "tails" writes how the situation could be looked at in a negative way. Share explanations, then critique and modify them so that both explanations are good examples.

- You are given a new puppy

- You are in a car crash that demolishes your car, but you are saved by your seatbelt with only a small cut on your arm

- Your new puppy dies unexpectedly in the night one week after you get it

- You're standing on the edge of the Grand Canyon counting your money, which is $500 in $100 bills; a gust of wind hits your hand and one of the $100 bills gets blown out over the canyon and drops thousands of feet and out of your sight

109

CHAPTER 12

So You Want to Change Somebody, Do You?

Everybody seems to want to change somebody. Parents want to change their kids. Kids want to change their parents. Teachers want to change their students and vice versa. Management wants to change labor and vice versa. Wives want to change their husbands and vice versa. Who do you want to change? Who is trying to change you?

At one time or another, we have all wanted to change people other than ourselves. We were sincere. We wanted to help them. We were sure that we knew what was good for them. We wanted to find some way to change them so that they would be happier, healthier, or in some way better than before. We had good motives and were often correct because we could see things they couldn't see; however, we usually weren't very successful. In fact, we were often hurt that the other person just could not see the logic of our argument. We were also astonished at the rigidity of the other person who refused to change in the direction that was so blatantly obvious to us. What went wrong?

First, think about how difficult it is for you to change some aspect of your own life. How many parts of your life do you know (or at least suspect) you should change? Haven't you thought about changes, like eating more nutritious food, getting more exercise, being more selective in the quantity and quality of television you watch, overcoming procrastination, and finding the positives in life rather than finding the negatives? Perhaps you have tried to give up addictions or change habits that involved tobacco, alcohol, sugar, salt, chocolate, caffeine, or relationships that you determined not to be in your best interest. You probably found it difficult to change yourself. It is even more difficult to change someone else. In fact, you probably can't change someone else—at least not for long.

A good rule to keep in mind is that a person can probably only change himself or herself. At least this is true if you want a change to continue. If a change is to continue over an extended period of time, any person doing the changing has to be internally convinced that the change is a good one. At some point this voluntary commitment has to be made. In other words, a change that will last will ultimately have to be seen by the "changer" as his or her voluntary choice.

People and organizations usually try one of four major ways to bring about change in others. They are the voluntary-considered approach, the voluntary-induced approach, the reluctant-coercive approach, and modeling the desired change.

Voluntary-Considered Approach

The voluntary-considered approach is built on the idea that the people doing the changing should make the choice *only after they have had the opportunity to consider all the facts available.* It is characterized by being as rational, objective, and scientific as possible. For example, if you were convinced that a member of your family should begin to get more exercise, your strategy would recognize that the ultimate choice lies with the family member, based on the best data possible. You would do your best to help provide all the "goods" and "bads" of making the change. You would supply data showing the probable benefits, such as feeling better, looking better, being healthier, and having increased self-esteem.

Even though you are convinced that the change to exercise more would be good, you would also furnish valid evidence supporting no change. You would be sure that your family member was aware of possible undesirable trade-offs of increased exercise, such as less time to do something else, some possible added expense, and some probable initial soreness. You would try to ensure that this decision would be made as scientifically as possible. You would not try to influence or manipulate the outcome. Both the negatives and the positives would be presented so that the family member would have all the facts possible. You would honestly try to "get all the cards on the table" because you believe that the decision should be made in the most rational way possible. You want your family member to be aware of all the downsides of the change, so he will have no negative surprises if he chooses to initiate the change. You realize that the decision might be that your family member will choose not to exercise more; however, you understand that the change, if initiated, will more likely be sustained because your family member would be convinced that the change would be worth it, and he would be intrinsically motivated to pursue it.

Although this approach represents the way that most people would like to be treated, it can involve large amounts of time to gather and sort through all the pros and cons. The other two formal approaches are faster but have their own shortcomings.

Voluntary-Induced Approach

The voluntary-induced approach to bring about change is characterized by persuasion, selling, and promoting. If you used this approach with your family member, you would try to sell him on the idea of getting more exercise. You would only stress the benefits of exercise. You would emphasize the physical and mental benefits. You would "stack the deck," so to speak, in favor of the change. You would deliberately suppress, ignore, or de-emphasize any data that would not favor the change. You might even offer a reward or a favor of some kind to initiate the change. Your strategy here is that you are only concerned with persuading him to start because once he gets more exercise, he will see and feel the benefits of it. Then he will be intrinsically motivated. This is a one-sided approach that does not prepare the changer for the problems that he might encounter as he attempts to change. He has only been shown the positive side of the picture. When he begins to experience the negatives, he might be less prepared to deal with them, have little success, lose motivation, and even give up. In addition, he may become angry with you for only giving one part of the evidence and "setting him up" to make the decision to change. He might see this approach as being deceptive. Finally, he might feel that you "conned" him into it, and it is at least partially your fault that it wasn't successful.

Reluctant-Coercive Approach

The reluctant-coercive approach is used when change is mandated, prescribed, commanded, or compelled even though the changer does not value the change. A person is coerced into a change because another person with real or implied power dictates it. The person who feels coerced into changing does not see the value of the change but begins it or "fakes it" because of the fear that the dictator will use some kind of power against him. For example, as a parent, you might dictate that your child should exercise more or you will not allow the child to watch television. Your child would not really value getting more exercise but would reluctantly do it in some minimal way in order to be able to watch television (note that a child would not have much power to use this approach successfully to coerce a parent into getting exercise). Also note that this approach requires the dictator to police the reluctant changer to make sure the change is carried out. It is very doubtful that your child would exercise when you, as the parent, were not present to verify that the exercise was done. Unless the changer is convinced of the value of the change to him, to the extent that he will do it when no one is watching, the change will probably have to be enforced.

The reluctant-coercive approach is often justified with the idea that the people who have to make the change would not try it unless they were forced to do so, but once they tried it, they would see its value and would become intrinsically motivated to sustain it. This might work in some cases, but there are many people who will rebel at any attempt to dictate any part of their lives. They would be so intent in defending any infringement of their personal freedom that they would probably never see the value of the change, no matter how much it improved their lives.

Another justification of this approach is that it is quick. This is not necessarily the case. Often what is seen as quick change is an initial compliance with the mandate that is not continued over the long run because the value of the change is seen by the dictator rather than by the person who has to implement the change. We are all familiar with the situation in which the change is implemented in a reluctant, half-hearted way and only to the degree that it will "look good" to the dictator. This minimal change may satisfy the dictator and give the impression that the change has been implemented even though its spirit and essence have not been.

Modeling is a powerful influence on change and is always in operation. This influence is the modeling behavior of the person or organization that is attempting to influence change. Actions have more influence than words. If you exercise regularly and I can see the benefits for you every day, you will have much more credibility as you encourage me to change my lifestyle to include more physical activity. In fact, if I see the benefits you receive from exercise, I might choose to start exercising on my own without any encouragement from you. On the other hand, couch potatoes do not have much credibility as spokespersons for exercise lifestyles. The same would be true of any advocate of a particular change.

Summary

Some of the most frustrated people in this world are people who are trying to change other people. The least frustrated ones are probably those who use change approaches that they would feel comfortable having used with them. Most of us do not want to be told what to do. Most of us do not want to be propagandized to make a decision about changing our lives on insufficient and manipulated evidence. *Most of us want to make our own decisions on the basis of all of the data available even though it might take more time.* Then, if we are really convinced of the value of the change, we are much more likely to seek out the knowledge necessary to bring it about, and we are more likely to expend the effort to sustain that change over a long period of time.

Perhaps the most realistic approach is not to even think about changing others in a manipulative sense. Maybe all we need to do is to "let the facts speak for themselves" and be valid role models of the desired behaviors. Modeling the desired behavior will give greater credibility to the advocates of the change. If we can't expect manipulation and coercion to bring about successful, long-term change, what other option do we have?

Doesn't it make sense that the person who has to implement and live with a change should have the opportunity to make that choice based on all of the evidence possible?

QUESTIONS

1. Which of the four change approaches (i.e., voluntary-considered, voluntary-induced, reluctant-coercive, or modeling) works best with you? That is, if someone wanted to help you change, which of the approaches or combination of approaches would you recommend that they use?

2. Which of the change approaches do you think is the least valuable in bringing about long-term change in somebody your age? Why do you make that choice? Which would be the next least valuable?

3. Do you think that the change approaches might work best if some are used in combination with others? Why or why not? Be sure to illustrate your answer with examples.

4. This question is especially related to the modeling approach. What is the name we use for a person who advocates that others do something but who does not do that thing himself or herself?

5. Can you think of times in your life when each of the approaches to help someone change was used to get you to change? As you look back on those times, what kinds of feelings do you remember having about each of those approaches when you experienced them?

ACTIVITIES

1. Can you think of times when someone else tried to get you to change? Were they successful? Based on the ideas in this chapter which approach, or combination of approaches, was used to get you to change?

2. Have individual members of your group or small groups each take one of the four change approaches. The objective is to list all possible advantages and disadvantages of that change approach. Then share your lists. Use group feedback to add to, delete from, or modify the lists to make them more complete and valid.

3. Have members of your group or small groups each take one of the four approaches used to change someone else. The objective is to plan a strategy using that approach to get Karl to eat a more nutritious diet. We want him to eat fewer fats, sugars, salt, and processed foods. We want him to eat more vegetables, fruits, grains, and non-processed foods. The strategies, based on each approach, should be shared with the total group to give information and to obtain feedback. Based on the feedback, each group should improve its strategy to make it a better example of the approach it was illustrating. Now have the class vote on which of the approaches or combination of approaches they would want to be used on them.

4. Perhaps you or your group could plan and conduct an experiment to see which of the approaches to changing someone are the most popular for a certain group of people.

119

Prepare a short description of each of the four approaches and either read them to others or have others read them. Then ask them which of the approaches they think would work best with them. You might want to begin with family, neighbors, and others who are geographically close and easy to interview. Whatever your results, remember that the results only apply to the group you ask and cannot be generalized to others. It is also a good idea to report your final results to those who participated.

5. Four approaches for getting someone to change have been listed here. Can you think of other approaches that should be added to the list? What are they? Are you sure they are not covered in these four? Obtain feedback from others. If it makes sense to do so, add them to the list and let others know so they also can make the addition to their lists.

CHAPTER 13

Little Things Can Mean a Lot

Many little things can add up to a big thing. A lot of little bricks can make a huge building. Get together enough single grains of sand and you can make a beach. A 1,000-mile walk has to begin with one step, and many steps must follow. In fact, everything in the world is made up of tiny little substances called molecules. *Being aware of the little things around you is probably as important as, if not more important than, being aware of the big things around you.*

Life is full of a lot of little things, and these things can make a big difference to you. For example, you just took a breath. This is a little thing that you do without thinking about it, but you can't skip many of these little breaths without some serious consequences. Your very life depends on these little breaths. The same thing is true about your heart. It might be interesting to you at this point to take some time to calculate how many times you breathe and how many times your heart beats in a lifetime. You will find some huge numbers representing those times. Those are little things, but they are very important to you. Because they seem so little, familiar, and insignificant to us, we often take them for granted. In the case of the lungs and heart, we not only take them for granted and ignore them but actually do things like smoking and eating unhealthy foods that harm them and eventually us. *We need to be more aware of these little things in our lives so that we can control them to make our lives better.*

The following are just some of the little things in your life and how they can mean a lot to you.

- If at age 20 you were to start putting only $1 a day into a savings fund that drew 10% compounded interest, and you never spent any of the money until age 65, you would be able to retire at that age with more than $260,000. One dollar a day is certainly not very much, but what a difference $260,000 would make to you when you retired.

- If you have a faucet in your house that leaks at the rate of one little drop per second, you would waste 900 gallons of water every year. Not only would that add to your personal expenses, but think of how much water that is wasted in a big city with the thousands, or even millions, of leaky faucets. If you have a leaky toilet, you could easily be losing 1,500 gallons of water per year. Like breathing and heartbeats, water is necessary to life, and we need to fix those little leaks and drips to help conserve this precious but taken-for-granted resource.

- What are some of the little things that you might do over a lifetime? Consider that you would do the things mentioned here every day over a 75-year period. What part of your total life would you use up doing that activity? If you took one minute each day to select and put on your shoes, or anything else that you do that takes one minute each day, you would use up about 29 days of your waking life, considering that you are awake 16 hours each day. What things do you do each day that take about a minute? Are they good uses of 29 days of your waking life?

- If you take four minutes each day to do something, you will be using up 116 days of your waking life to do it. What do you do each day that takes about four minutes? Are these wise uses of 116 days of your life?

- What kinds of things do you do for about 13 minutes a day? Really think about this one, because this amount of time each day adds up to about one full year of your waking life. Think of what you can do in a whole year of 16-hour days!

- Some people watch television a lot. If you watch television for an average of two hours a day for 75 years, you will spend approximately 8.5 years of 16-hour days of your life just doing that. That means that a full 12.5% of your life would be spent watching television. If you are one of those people who watches an average of four hours of television per day, you will spend 25% of your waking life watching whatever it is that you watch on television. That amounts to about 19 years of your life! Is that the best use of one-fourth of your life?

- It takes 3,500 calories to become a pound of weight for human beings. That means that if you ate just one extra tortilla chip (approximately 10 calories) each day and changed nothing else in your life, you would gain a pound of weight in less than a year. In 25 years you would gain more than 25 pounds. A little thing like a tortilla chip can add up very quickly. And who ever ate only one chip?

- On the other hand, what if you added a one mile walk (about 100 calories) each day to your lifestyle? At this rate, you would lose a pound about every 35 days if you did nothing else in your life differently. In a year's time you could lose approximately 10.5 pounds.

- If you make the little choice to have your one cup of potato baked, it will have 118 calories, but if you have the same amount of potato as French fries, it will have 456 calories. Small decision, big difference.

- Remember earlier that you could save $1 a day and make more than $260,000.00 when you retired? If you spent the $1 a day instead, you would spend $15,425 in the same time period. A little thing like making a decision to be saving or spending $1 a day can really mean a lot in a few years.

- If you bought a soft drink or coffee and it cost you $1.75 each day, you would pay out a little less than $32,000 over a 50-year period.

Other things that are little when looked at individually but that can add up to a person feeling good about himself or herself are:

- A little smile from someone can change a whole day; so can a frown, but the change is to a different kind of day.

- A kind little word of praise or acknowledgment can change a bad day into a good one.

- A little thing like a soft touch on the shoulder can make a person feel better when he or she is down.

- A little inexpensive and unexpected gift can make a person feel very important and needed.

There are many more examples that could be used to show how little things can mean a lot. Perhaps you can think of some.

If you want to have more control over your life, one of the best ways is to look for the little things in life that make a big difference. Little things can be found in the area of money management where small amounts of money earning interest over long periods of time can result in a lot of savings. Little things can be found in the area of physical health where wellness is paying attention to the many small habits we have in nutrition, weight control, and exercise. Even small things like the ways we talk to ourselves and to others can make big differences in our mental health and our relationships.

Little things can mean a lot—a lot of good or a lot of bad.

It makes sense to look out for the little things because they can add up quickly.

QUESTIONS

1. What little things in your life can you think of which can add up and have a big influence on your life? For example, a few extra calories each day can add many pounds to your body over the years.

2. There was a song many years ago entitled "Little Things Mean a Lot." Do you believe that? If so, give some examples. If not, why not?

3. In terms of human relationships, what sorts of little things mean a lot to you? What little things can someone do to, for, or with you that make you feel happy?

4. Beginning to save even small amounts of money at an early age can result in large amounts of money later in life. Have you started a savings plan of some type? If you haven't, find out who has the expertise to show you how much you could save if you started saving immediately, even though what you save is a small amount.

5. Many of the little things we do that can add up to be good or bad for us are called "habits." What kinds of habits do you have that you should keep? What habits do you have that you should replace? Which habit should you replace first because it could hurt you the most?

ACTIVITIES

1. Think of some common thing that you do every day. Now calculate how much time you would spend in your waking lifetime if you lived until 80 years of age (hint: you will need to remember when you started doing the activity and use 16 hours for your waking hours each day). How many minutes, hours, days, months, or years of your waking life will that activity have taken when you are 80 years old? Is that a good use of your life? Is there some way you want to change this part of your life to have time to do other things?

2. Calculate how many days you have lived. Now calculate how many more days you can reasonably expect to live. What percentage of your expected life have you lived? What percentage of your total life do you expect to live? Are there any changes you want to make in your life to make it better in the time you have left?

3. Can you construct a picture, cartoon, model, collage, or other non-verbal way to illustrate how little things can mean a lot?

4. What one "little" thing could you start doing today, and continue to do the rest of your life, that would in some way make you better or happier?

CHAPTER 14

It's Okay—Everybody Makes Mistakes

Splash!! The glass of juice spilled all over the table. As I jumped up to get a dishcloth to wipe it up, I saw my granddaughter with eyes and mouth wide open looking at me in stark terror. The fear gave way momentarily to a silent plea for mercy.

"It's okay," I said. "Everybody makes mistakes." Nicole's face immediately changed to a look of relief, then to a look of inquisitiveness which, in turn, was replaced by a look of combined understanding and relief.

"That's right," she said as she helped to clean up the mess. "Everybody does make mistakes."

This very bright six-year-old had not yet learned a truism about her species. She somehow learned that making mistakes is considered "bad" and that when she makes a mistake she is bad and probably needs some kind of punishment. The truth is that it is natural for us humans to make mistakes.

Mistakes are natural. There is no way that a human being can live in this world without making some kinds of

129

mistakes. This is especially true of explorers and adventurers, which is what kids are. Kids don't make mistakes, at least not in their eyes, while they are still young. They are just exploring the "stuff" around them. To them, the $100 gift vase from Aunt Rose is just an attractive object that needs to be picked up, touched, smelled, maybe licked, and eventually discarded after the inspection. There is no dollar amount or sentimental value placed on this vase by the child. The vase just "is." That vase, however, represents monetary value and the fond memories of Aunt Rose to the child's parents. If the accidental dropping of the vase occurs, quick punishment is administered, and a lesson about being "bad" is learned. The child's lesson is that picking up interesting objects can be a mistake. Dropping them is an even bigger mistake. This is just one instance of how the natural tendencies of exploration by a child can be interpreted as a mistake or "crime" by an adult. This is also how children can learn that trying to find out about this wonderful world in which they live is a dangerous undertaking and should be avoided. Sitting in front of the television for mind-numbing hours, however, is soon found to be safe and "good" in most homes.

The same thing happens with adolescents and adults. When you believe that a mistake is something bad, you go out of your way to make sure to avoid any situation where you can make a "bad mistake" again. People who find it difficult to do and say the "correct things" become shy and avoid people. People who take a little longer to understand math classes might feel "slow" and consequently avoid math classes as they go through school. People who try to play a new sport but are concerned that their natural mistakes as beginners are making them look stupid often give up trying to learn the new sport. The key to this problem is that mistakes are part of the natural consequences of living and trying. *The problem is not that you make a mistake, but it is how you interpret the "mistake."*

How should we treat mistakes? One approach is to consider them as a natural part of learning. What we call a mistake is really just an unsuccessful attempt or the valuable discovery that something does not work. For example, if you have ever locked yourself out of your house, you have had to test hypotheses about which doors or windows might be unlocked. You tried some windows and doors first because you believed they were most likely to be unlocked. Even if you found they were all locked, that was good information that you used to start a new direction in your investigation of how to get into the house. Even the very act of getting locked out of your house need not be considered a mistake. You could simply think of it as a temporarily inconvenient situation that taught you always to carry your house keys with you, to hide extra keys, or to leave a key with your neighbors for such an emergency.

Perhaps it is a good idea not even to use the word "mistake" in your thinking or speech. You would be wise to think to yourself that you didn't make a mistake, but you:

- discovered something that didn't work

- tried an idea, but it failed

- had an unsuccessful attempt

- acted on a reasonable guess, but it didn't work

- disproved your hypothesis

- had a learning experience of what not to do

Note that the phrasing used above as substitutions for thinking about "mistakes" avoids the implications of any guilt or of doing anything wrong. They simply describe situations that happen to anyone who is alive and active.

The only way that you can feel guilty or wrong is if you allow yourself to think that way. Think of life as a continual exploration or adventure in which you do not make mistakes.

You have learning experiences.

QUESTIONS

1. Do you believe that "mistakes are a natural and expected part of living"?

2. Can you think of times in your early life when you were punished for doing something that was interpreted as bad, but you were only being inquisitive?

3. Can you think of any things or situations you avoid because you are fearful that you might make a mistake? Do you think you might behave differently if you adopted the idea that mistakes are really valuable learning opportunities that make you a wiser person as a result?

4. It has been said that it is all right to make a mistake once or perhaps even two times, but that it is not all right to make the same mistake three or more times. What does that mean to you?

5. If you take the advice in this chapter and do not use the word "mistake," what word or phrase would you use?

6. How might thinking of yourself as an explorer in life change the way you deal with what some people call mistakes?

ACTIVITIES

1. Create a description of a situation in which a character gets in some kind of trouble because a person in power (boss, teacher, parent, etc.) interprets the character's actions as a mistake that is bad. Now create the same situation, but have the person in power believe that it is okay to make a mistake because the character can learn from it. Share these creations with others in your group. What differences occurred with the characters whose actions were treated as mistakes and those whose actions were treated as learning experiences?

2. Make a list of times in your life when you have made what some people call mistakes. In how many of the situations did you think of this feedback as being bad or embarrassing in some way? In how many of the situations did you treat the feedback as a learning experience? What did you learn from each of these situations? Did you change any of your actions as a result of what you learned? Did you ever repeat any of these "mistakes"?

3. In your own words, write out the three most important ideas you learned from this chapter.

4. Illustrate (cartoon, painting, drawing, etc.) a situation in which someone learns a valuable lesson when he or she makes a "mistake."

CHAPTER 15

A Different Look at Goals

"Goals" simply describe something you desire. They give direction and meaning to your life if they are chosen with care. Think for a minute about your present goals.

You should have both long-term and short-term goals. If you only have long-term goals, you are more likely to become frustrated as you strive over a long period of time before the goal is achieved. For example, if you were working toward a college degree, it would probably take at least four years to attain this goal. The trick is to combine compatible short-term goals and long-term goals. Short-term goals are completed in less time and give the feeling of accomplishment. Using the same example of attending college, you would think of each week, each paper, and each test as a successful step toward your eventual degree and be proud of those short-term accomplishments.

Daily goals, often in the form of lists-to-remember-and-do, can promote even more specific short-term success and subsequent motivation. Still using the same example of college, every time you go to class, write down important ideas in your notes, participate in discussions, complete assignments, or accomplish anything on your list, you would be getting that much closer to your ultimate goal and you would be reinforced with each accomplishment. Note that if you only have short-term goals and they do not have a focus, you risk getting a lot done without making any progress. Don't confuse "being busy" with "accomplishments." As you work out your goals, make sure that you include daily and short-term goals as well as the long-term ones. You need the long-term goals to give you direction, whereas you need the short-term ones to complete the everyday tasks or to obtain feedback about corrections that need to be made.

There are several kinds of goals. The most commonly discussed goals are those that I am calling "achieve-a-dream goals." These are very specific goals in which you clearly visualize your achievement of something. These goals can be anything from the receipt of a college degree to purchasing a home overlooking the ocean. You have probably dreamed of having a date with a certain person, owning a certain car, having a certain kind of look, living in a certain place, or becoming in some way very rich and famous. These are your personal dreams and when you deliberately decide that you are going to set out to accomplish them, they become your long-term goals. There is a logical set of steps that you can take to accomplish goals of this kind.

- **Write out your goal** in specific terms so that it creates for you a clear and precise mental picture of you attaining it. For example, on January 1, 20XX, I will proudly look in the mirror to see a (describe exactly how you want to see yourself) body that has a healthy blend of strength, endurance, and flexibility as the result of the lifestyle changes I am beginning today.

- **Ask yourself WHY** this goal is important enough for you to spend your time and energy pursuing it. As a priority in your life, does it warrant the time and effort to achieve it?

- **Ask yourself HOW** you will go about attaining your dream.

    1. What factors will promote its accomplishment?

    2. What factors will hinder its accomplishment?

    3. What new knowledge and skills will you need?

    4. Who else will you need to help you accomplish it?

    5. What specific step-by-step plan will you follow?

- **Begin the first step** in your plan.

Any good book or article on goals or success can give more detailed ways to accomplish your achieve-a-dream goals. I want to use the rest of this chapter to discuss aspects of goals as well as goals that are seldom examined.

About this point in the chapter, you might be feeling uneasy. You may have gotten the impression that you must have an all-consuming goal as described above or you will never be successful. You should not feel that way. Perhaps the most important thing I can tell you is that it is okay if you do not have a strongly held goal at this time. You should not feel guilty or inadequate if you don't have a compelling drive to accomplish some dream. This doesn't mean that you shouldn't have such a dream; it just means that there are times in everyone's life when it is normal not to be driven by an intensely pursued goal.

There will be times when you have accomplished a major goal and have not yet discovered your new dream. Again, don't feel guilty or at a loss. Instead, shift to "exploration" as your goal. This means that you will not have a single focus, but will deliberately set about to explore a new variety of things. You deliberately seek experiences you never did before, visit places you never visited before, talk to people you never talked to before, eat foods you have never eaten before, and more. Your goal is to have as many first-time experiences as you can. This is a time when you can add some adventure into your life. What sort of unusual thing might you do that would qualify as an adventure? My grade school principal celebrated his 80th birthday with his first parachute jump. It is never too late for you to explore this fascinating world in which we live. During these explorations, you might find something that is so enthralling that you make some part of it your next achieve-a-dream goal. Perhaps a lifetime of exploration makes sense to you. Exploration goals could be a predominant part of your life. Such goals could occupy the interludes between your single-focus goals, or they could be interspersed within your daily or weekly goals throughout your life. Don't just think outside the box; live outside the box.

An interesting approach is to mix long-term, single-focus goals with exploration goals. In this way, you would have a long-term goal for which you would be striving, but you wouldn't be so focused on it that you would miss some exploratory expeditions along the way. Think of it as analogous to driving a car from one town to another. You could, with singleness of purpose, get in your car and drive at the speed limit straight from one town to the other without taking your eyes from the road; however, another approach would be to look at a map and see if there might not be some interesting places along the way. By exploring these places, the trip could be much more interesting without a significant loss of time.

This might be an approach to life that you should consider. Are you perhaps so intent on the destinations in your life that you don't enjoy the journeys? Are there adventures that you are missing because you are focusing so intently on a particular goal? Are you sure there isn't time on your present journey to talk with the child, admire the sunset, listen to the birds, paint the picture, write the poem, pet the dog, take a quiet walk, or do something you want to do just for the pleasure or adventure of it?

Another kind of goal might be called "time-to-enjoy" goals. These are goals planned to ensure that the achieve-a-dream goals are really enjoyed. It sometimes happens that people will strive to achieve a dream and be disappointed and feel let down when they finally achieve it. This may be because they don't take the time to enjoy the fruits of their labors. They achieve the long-sought goal and then go on to another goal without enjoying the first achievement. You want to be sure that you set aside time to enjoy the goals that you achieve. Take some time to enjoy the house you worked so hard to get. Take some time off from your work and spend some quality time with the children you were so anxious to have. Take some time to spend some of the money you earn on yourself and those you love. *Most goals are nothing more than ways to make you happier in some way. Make sure that you take the time to enjoy that happiness.*

Another (and perhaps the most important) goal is that of enjoying every day to the fullest. Living every day to the fullest is an ever-present goal that can keep the single-minded strivers from losing sight of the fact that the present moment is the only one we have, and we need to make the best of it. Like all short-term goals, however, it needs to be tempered with the caution that *only* thinking of the present can have negative consequences to yourself and others in the long-term. Perhaps the best advice is to live for the moment without sacrificing the future for yourself or others. For example, a person who gets drunk at a bar and then tries to drive home is living in the moment but is being totally irresponsible in regard to the possible negative consequences to his or her future and the future of others. Nevertheless, many of us do not enjoy the present moment. We often find ourselves wasting our present moments by trying to retrieve the irretrievable past or by worrying about the future. We can deliberately be more conscious of the present moment. We can be more aware of the sights, sounds, smells, textures, and tastes that surround us. Most of us need to focus on finding more enjoyment in our daily experiences of being.

Consider the following statements regarding goals:

- If you don't have a goal, you won't know when you get there because you won't know where you are going.

- If you think goals are unimportant, remember that it takes just as much energy to run around in circles as it does to run in a straight line.

- Once you have a goal clearly in mind, your subconscious will begin to work on ways to achieve it even though you are doing something unrelated. You have probably had the experience of thinking of the answer to a problem at a time when you weren't consciously thinking of the problem.

- Deciding on a goal and making a commitment to it is one of the most difficult things that people do. It is difficult because we are often afraid that we could be choosing a poor goal or that we will not be able to achieve it.

- Goals should always be stated in a positive form that gives a clear mental picture of that which is desired. Goals should be clear indicators of where you want to go, not from where you are leaving. Goals need to state what you are gaining, not what you are giving up.

- Many writers admonish their readers to include both starting and ending dates in their goal statements. It makes sense to include both. You have to start sometime, but the ending date should be thought of as a target only, not as an absolute.

Goals have changed over the centuries and are different among cultures. In the past or even today in less-developed countries with subsistence economies, the goals were clear. People in these situations knew that they must get up in the morning and nearly all of their time would be spent attaining the necessities of life. Contrast this with most young people in developed countries or wealthy families. They have their basic needs more than met. There is little for them to do and even less for them to do that has meaning to them! Some of us have goals that only pursue "stuff," like electronic gadgets, designer clothes, and the latest form of entertainment. *Helping people, especially young people, create meaningful goals is a major challenge of our times.*

Your life is in many ways a series of journeys and destinations that you first plan and then take. Goals are important to having successful journeys. You have to decide what your destination will be, why you want to get there, what routes you will take, when you will leave, and when you plan to arrive.

Make sure to plan your journeys to be as enjoyable as your destinations.

QUESTIONS

1. Do you have some achieve-a-dream goals? What are they? Have you written out these dreams as goals in specific terms? If not, why don't you do that right now? You will seldom achieve a goal that is not specific and clear. Use the suggested form in the example if you don't have your own format.

2. Do you see any potential problems with "exploration" goals? Under what circumstances could they become problematic?

3. Do you see any potential problems with the "time-to-enjoy" goals? Under what circumstances could they become problematic?

4. What is the idea behind the sentence, "It takes just as much energy to run around in circles as it does to run in a straight line"?

5. What reasons are there to state a goal in the positive form?

ACTIVITIES

1. If you have not done so already, write down one of your achieve-a-dream goals in specific terms as suggested in the chapter. Does your written goal give you a mental picture of yourself at a certain time in the future having achieved the goal? Now go on to the next steps. Why do you want to gain this? How important is it in your life when you compare it to other things you could be doing if you didn't pursue this goal? Will it give you only short-term pleasure or might it be valuable to you in the long-term?

2. Explain the relationships between short-term and long-term goals. Be sure to include the ideas of feelings of accomplishment, motivation, and keeping focus. Share your explanations in the group and refine them based on the feedback from others.

3. Explain what the exploration goal is and how it works. Be sure to include in your explanation the ideas of its use between achieve-a-dream goals, as a goal in and of itself, and as part of a combination. Again, share and refine with others.

4. What are some exploration goals that you have? List those things that you haven't done before but would like to try. What is stopping you? Is there one of them (or part of one of them) that you could complete in the near future if you really concentrated on it? Choose one and

set a date. Share your goal with others. Maybe someone would like to do it with you.

5.   Think of someone you know who always seems to be working and seldom stops or slows down to enjoy life. How would you explain to him or her the premise of time-to-enjoy goals? Maybe it would be a good idea to do just that and talk to the person if you feel comfortable doing it. How can you talk to the person so that he or she accepts your suggestion as kind and helpful?

6.   Create two original situations that illustrate someone who is violating the idea that you should live in the moment without sacrificing the future for yourself or others. Create one situation in which the person sacrifices his or her future and one situation in which the person sacrifices the future of someone else. Share these with others in your group and then discuss what relationship you believe these scenarios have with the idea of responsibility.

7.   Explain in your own words all of your reasons for having clear goals. Share those reasons with the group. Add to your list as new reasons are contributed.

8.   Using the analogy of an airplane pilot flying for one of the commercial airlines, illustrate the appropriate uses of goals as suggested in this chapter. Use as many ideas about goals as possible. When you share your analogy

with others in your group, be sure to improve your paper based on the feedback you receive.

9. "Helping people, especially young people, to find meaningful goals is a major challenge of our time," is a statement in this chapter. Do you agree with the statement or not? Explain your answer. Even if you disagree, what would you suggest as meaningful and realistic goals for young people to have and pursue? Share these in the group. Would there be any one or more of these suggestions that you could help get started?

10. Make a visual illustration of taking one of your goals from the starting point of stating it in specific terms through all the steps that are necessary to achieve it. Show your illustration to others and see if they can think of steps you should add or other modifications that would improve it.

11. Are there any of the ideas about goals that are especially easy to illustrate with a picture, cartoon, or other visual medium?

CHAPTER 16
On Being Responsible

Responsible behavior could be defined as "doing what you believe to be correct even when no one else is looking." Another way to define responsible behavior might be that it is "deliberate behavior that will help you get what you want without harming your future or the future of others." So if you are a responsible person, you will do things that help you get what you want now but won't hinder getting what you want later. You also will act in ways that won't harm other people now or in the future. You will be so committed to responsible behavior that you will behave responsibly, even when there is no one watching.

For example, if you were the responsible driver of a car, you would stop at stop signs and obey the speed limit even when there were no police to be seen. You would stop at the signs and obey the speed limits because not obeying could put you and others in dangerous situations that could cause many kinds of physical, financial, and mental problems. These problems could have negative effects on you and others in the future as well as in the present.

Another example of responsible behavior would be deciding to exercise every day for an hour. You always do the prescribed activities even when you don't feel like it that day, and you do it even though no one is there to make sure that you do it. You don't cheat yourself by doing fewer minutes of exercise or doing a smaller number of repetitions when you think no one is looking. You run or walk because you know that you look better, feel better, and are generally healthier if you exercise properly. You know that you will be helping yourself greatly as you get older by starting good habits now. You will also be setting a great example for others. And you aren't causing harm to anyone.

If you choose to act responsibly using the approach described here, you will want to get into the habit of asking yourself some questions about the human consequences of your actions each time you think through a decision. The basic questions would be:

1. Is what I want really important?

2. Will this action really help me get what I want?

3. If I do this, how will it affect me in the future?

4. If I do this, how will it affect other people now and in the future?

If all the human consequences could be predicted to be positive from answering the questions above, then you would act on your decision. For example, if you wanted to be healthier and change from the habit of smoking cigarettes to the habit of only putting the cleanest available air in your lungs, you could go through the questions. Your answers would probably be something like this:

1. Yes, it is certainly important to be healthy. Without my health, I am restricted in my life and the ways I can be productive and happy.

2. Yes, it is important for me to put the cleanest available air in my lungs. The scientific evidence is clear on this. I will undoubtedly be healthier if I put clean air in my lungs than if I put contaminated air from cigarette smoke in my lungs.

3. My future will be more positive in that I should live longer and better because I should have fewer diseases and other problems associated with cigarette smoking. As a healthier person, I can live a fuller, higher quality life.

4. Everyone who is close to me will be better off in many well-known ways as a result of my switching from the habit of smoking cigarettes to only breathing the cleanest air available. The only people who could be hurt by my decision would be those who grow, manufacture, or distribute tobacco products.

With this kind of overwhelming evidence, it is easy to make the switch to putting clean air in your lungs, even though the actual switching might be difficult.

You can easily see what a responsible decision would look like if you were doing the opposite and trying to decide if you should switch from putting clean air in your lungs to putting cigarette smoke in your lungs. It would, again, be a very important decision in your life, but every question would uncover major potential negative effects on your health now and in the future, as well as similar negative outcomes for other people now and in the future. Your only responsible decision would be *not* to start smoking.

A very difficult aspect of acting responsibly occurs when some of the four questions are answered in the positive and others are answered in the negative. Then it becomes a matter of having to weigh and balance the positive and negative. Perhaps the major criterion for judging the best decision would then be: "Which decision results in the most positive total human consequences when you consider the long-term as well as the short-term?" That is, the most responsible decision is the one that generates, even if only marginally, the most positive human consequences now and in the long run.

The following are some further ideas about responsibility:

- Responsible people want to control their own lives but do not want to control the lives of other people.

- Responsible people want to achieve their own goals but not at the expense of others.

- Responsible decisions are based on facts, reality, and the best data available, not on opinions, hearsay, innuendo, or the like.

- Responsible people think in terms of the consequences of their actions for the future as well as for the short-term.

- Responsible people accept responsibility for their behavior. They make their decisions deliberately and with as much care as possible, and then accept the consequences of their actions. They do not offer alibis or look for scapegoats.

- Responsible people are self-disciplined. They do what they believe must be done, and they do it even when nobody is looking. Conversely, they do what they believe must be done even though everybody else is doing the opposite and there is great peer pressure to conform.

- Responsible people are self-disciplined with their time. They do what needs to be done *when* it must be done; they don't procrastinate.

- Responsible people are realistic. For example, they know that the world "just is" and that they construct their unique, personal sets of beliefs, emotions, and feelings on how they interpret this world. They accept the fact that others also construct their beliefs, emotions, and feelings based on their unique interpretations of the world. As a result, they expect that they often will have different beliefs, emotions, and feelings about the same people, objects, and events. These differences are accepted as natural and become part of their decision-making process.

- People who consistently act responsibly feel good about themselves. Responsible behavior not only builds self-esteem, but it also tends to draw recognition and respect from others.

- Responsible people do the best with what they have; they do not despair because of what they never had or what they might have lost.

- Responsible people don't dwell in the past. They know that the past is water under the bridge, and they don't waste their precious lives worrying about what could have been or should have been.

- Responsible people tend to live lives of balance and moderation. They are careful how they use all kinds of resources. They are concerned not to take more than their fair share.

- Responsible people pull their own weight. They plan and conduct their lives so they are not a burden to others.

- Responsible people treat other people as if they were also responsible. They treat others as responsible until others prove themselves to be irresponsible.

- Responsible behavior is probably the best measure of mature behavior.

Parents, schools, and all human service agencies should consider the teaching of responsible behavior to be one of the highest of all priorities. Responsible people make the important decisions in their lives. They do not give others control over their lives unless there is not enough time to get needed information or the information is too technical for them to understand. They consider expert advice as hypotheses or alternatives to be used in making their own decisions. Even though they might solicit advice and ideas from others, such as medical doctors and financial planners, they always become personally as knowledgeable as possible because they know that they alone will make the final decision and they alone will have to live with the consequences.

One of the best ways to teach responsible behavior is to model it.

QUESTIONS

1. What is your personal definition of responsible behavior? Do you agree with the definitions in the chapter? Can you give an original example of responsible behavior from your own life?

2. What would be your definition of irresponsible behavior? Give an original example that you have personally observed.

3. Can you think of any irresponsible behavior that you have done in the past? Why was it irresponsible? Do you continue to do this behavior? Why or why not?

4. Can you think of something you have done that you think is especially responsible behavior? What makes you most proud of this behavior?

5. There is a list of ideas about responsibility in the chapter. Do you agree with all of them? Do you disagree with any of them? If so, why?

6. What ideas would you want to add to the list of ideas about responsibility?

7. Who do you know that consistently acts responsibly? Why do you say so? Does he or she act in accordance with the four questions cited in the chapter?

8. How would you have to change to become more responsible?

9. Can you think of a situation in which responsible behavior would be "doing what you think is right even though everybody else is doing the opposite"?

10. Do you believe it is necessary to consider the consequences to others in order to make a responsible decision? Why or why not?

ACTIVITIES

1. Using the four questions about the human consequences of making a responsible decision, apply them to a real decision that you think you need to make. You are trying to act responsibly, using the questions as a guide. If you can't think of a real personal decision, perhaps you can choose from the following list: whether to drop out of high school, get married before completing high school, do anything that is illegal, buy a $2,500 watch, or spend the money your parents saved for your education to buy a new sports car.

2. In your mind's eye, look around your school, neighborhood, and community. Write down some examples of irresponsible behavior that you have observed. With the class or with small groups, record a master list of observed irresponsible behaviors. Does everyone agree that each of the behaviors is properly classified as irresponsible? Why do you classify these actions as irresponsible? How do your choices of irresponsible behavior compare to the four questions above? Share your answers with your class.

3. Using the same process as in the previous activity, make individual lists of responsible behavior that you have observed in your school, neighborhood, and community. Again, as a group or total class, make a master list and answer the questions about your choices.

4. Using your master list of irresponsible behaviors from the activity above, choose three that seem especially troublesome. Now describe how a person would have to

behave in order to change the irresponsible behavior into responsible behavior. What different way or ways of thinking would be necessary for the new, responsible behavior to be adopted?

5. Create a story about a person your age who acts responsibly and does what he or she believes to be right even though there is peer pressure to act irresponsibly. For example, the driver of a car will not take a drink even though all the other people in the car are drinking and encouraging the driver to drink with them. Share your stories with others in your group or class.

6. Using the list of further ideas about responsibility, choose one of the ideas. Write at least one original example of that idea being properly practiced. Share the examples in your small group or with the total class. Be sure that the examples are consistent with the idea.

7. Discuss the question, "What is the most difficult thing about consistently behaving in a responsible way?"

CHAPTER 17

Ask "Why" Before You Ask "How"

One simple way to gain more control over your life is to ask the correct questions at the correct times. Everything that you do in your life has at least two basic parts to it. One part is the reason why you should do it. The other part is how you can do it. If you determine that it is important, then you should learn the best way to complete it. Simply put, you should ask "why" questions before you ask "how" questions.

Asking "why" questions first can save you a lot of time, energy, money, and grief. Perhaps the first rule about working smarter, not harder, is that you should always determine whether what you are about to do is worth doing. This is especially true of key decisions in your life involving such things as marriage, housing, children, religion, politics, insurance, transportation, education, friendships, entertainment, and wealth.

"Why" questions can be asked in different forms. Some of those approaches are expressed in the following questions:

- Why should I do that?

- Should I do that?

- What is the best thing to do?

- Is that the most important thing to do?

- Do I have a good rationale (reason) for doing this?

- Why am I doing this?

The *why* questions are so important because they are the first questions you ask and they help you form the goals that are the focus of all subsequent actions. Answering the *why* questions first accomplishes several things such as:

- ***Helping you clarify your objectives.*** They force you into more detailed, specific thinking about the importance of goals to which you might dedicate energy, time, and other resources.

- ***Forcing you to think of alternatives.*** When you are thinking about the importance of doing something, you automatically have to think of alternatives with which to compare it. Sometimes an alternative will prove to be superior to the original idea.

- ***Giving you a different perspective.*** We often decide to do something because everyone else seems to be doing it; we don't look at it from our own personal perspective. Doing something only because everybody else is doing it is a terrible rationale.

- ***Increasing your productivity.*** If you question what you are doing and choose to do the most important things, you are more productive. You eliminate many of the low-priority things in your life and focus your energy on the things you have decided to be of higher priority.

- ***Forcing you to think about consequences.*** Many times we do something without looking realistically at what the consequences will be to us or to other people. If I ask myself, "Should I get a pet dog?" I will need to determine who will take care of it, who will pay for its expenses, and how happy the dog will be, among other things.

One question that comes up in just about everyone's life concerns the purchase of a new car. Imagine that this thought has just come into your mind. Being a bright person, you ask, "Why do I need a new car?" before you ask yourself, "How can I get a new car?" Instead of rushing to the new car agency, you think seriously about the alternatives to the purchase of the new car. You might find that you don't really need any kind of car. Your thinking might reveal that the only reason that you considered a new car was that you wanted to impress people, and you reject that as a good reason to spend your money on a new car. You might discover that you value a car only as transportation and that buying a used one will save you money you can use for better purposes. You might determine that your present car is nearing automotive death and that a different used car would be a much better alternative for you. Of course, you might be wealthy and determine that you can easily afford a new car, it is the best way to fulfill your transportation needs at this time, and that you would really "look good" driving it. First you have to decide what is important to you; then you start planning how to get it.

Another example involves answering the question, "Why do I need designer clothes?" before you ask, "How can I get designer clothes?" Many people who answer this question honestly find that they want designer clothes because their friends wear them and they want to look like their friends. The clothes are not necessarily of better quality or superior design, but they usually are much more expensive than similar clothes without the designer labels. Many people don't ask why and just unthinkingly follow the crowd and pay extra money to be dressed like everybody else.

"How to do something" is very important and necessary in any undertaking, but it must follow the "why should I do something" questions to ensure that the undertaking has value. Too much of our time is wasted doing things that we wouldn't do if we took a little time to think about them. The habit of taking a few minutes to ask *why* first could save years, even total lives, from being spent in unfulfilling toil to achieve unquestioned and irrelevant goals.

Ask WHY first; then ask HOW.

QUESTIONS

1. Can you think of a time in your life in which you did something that caused you some harm or unhappiness? Could you have prevented the "bad" outcome if you had asked, "Why should I do this?" before you did it? Why didn't you ask *why*?

2. Can you think of real-life situations (or perhaps fictional situations) in which someone should have asked *why* before he or she did something that turned out to be undesirable?

3. Have you ever done something because everyone else was doing it without really questioning whether it should be done? For example, many of the habits we have are the result of seeing others doing them, and we simply accept them as the natural thing to do without truly questioning their value. Habits can be good ones (such as frequent exercise and looking for the positive in people), or they can be bad ones that can harm you (such as smoking and looking for the worst in others). Describe a habit you have now that was not really chosen by you in a deliberate way. Has the habit turned out to be good for you or not?

4. Can you think of situations in which it might be best for you to act first and then think about it later? Explain.

ACTIVITIES

1. Create a short story in which someone's actions get them into trouble because they concentrated *how* to do something before they questioned *why* it was important. If you cannot think of a situation quickly, you might want to create a story that involves health, safety, personal relationships, or the law.

2. Discuss with others the following statement: "Asking why you should do something before you do it is nothing more than trying to predict the consequences of your actions before you act." Do you believe that is a true statement? If so, why? If not, why not?

3. Can you think of a situation in which your actions might be good for you but might bring harm to someone else?

4. Can you think of a situation in which your actions might have good consequences for others but bad consequences for you?

5. What do you think is the possible reason or reasons that some people seldom seem to question themselves about why they do things?

6. Asking *why* is a way of discovering what is important to you. In the following list, rank the five things that are most important to you. Be prepared to explain your answers.

162

a) A pet of your choice that will be your companion for life

b) A very physically attractive mate who thinks you are the most magnificent creature on earth

c) A $100,000 annual salary guaranteed for life

d) A job that you really love to do guaranteed for life

e) That you are very physically attractive for the rest of your life

f) That you have very good physical health for the rest of your life

g) A new automobile of your choice every year for the rest of your life

h) Having excellent mental health for the rest of your life

i) Finding joy and happiness in your everyday life

j) Owning a house that all of your friends envy

k) Having several good friends whom you can trust

l) A lifetime pass to see any movie any time you decide to go

m) A mate who is smart, fun to be with, and makes $100,000 a year

n) A family that enjoys one another and provides security for each other

o) Owning an island in the Caribbean and having $10 million to fix the island as you wish

CHAPTER 18

I Win, You Win, Everybody Wins

The process of coming to an agreement is what is commonly called negotiating. Although negotiating is usually connected with business (labor and management negotiate) and government (the United States and Russia negotiate), we all do it every day. Parents and their children negotiate, teachers and students negotiate, spouses negotiate, brothers and sisters negotiate, and speeders might even try to negotiate with police officers. Think of all the times in the last few days when you have been involved in a negotiation with one or more people where you were trying to come to an agreement. How did you go about reaching those agreements? What were the results of those agreements? Negotiated agreements fall into three categories: lose-lose, win-lose, and win-win.

Lose-lose is a decision that results in *everyone being a loser.* For example, you own a business, and I work for you. I ask you for a large raise in salary. You tell me that you cannot afford a large raise because you are not making enough profit. You tell me that my raise will cause the company to go out of business. I demand the raise anyway because I don't believe you, and I am the only person who can do the job. You are forced to give me the huge raise. In a few weeks the company has to go out of business. We both lose. I lose my job, and you lose your business. *Most lose-lose situations result from a lack of trust, rigidly-held positions, a lack of information, and not predicting long-term consequences.*

Win-lose is a decision that results in *someone winning and someone losing.* Races, games, trials, voting, and awards are good examples of when one person or one group wins and everyone else loses. This results in some people being happy and some people being unhappy. If I beat you in a game of checkers I will be happy, and you will probably be at least somewhat unhappy. At an award assembly at school the few people getting the awards will probably be happy, but all the rest of the students might feel like losers. *Any time there is a competition there will likely be one or just a few winners and many losers.*

An everyday example of a win-lose situation is a brother and sister who find the last apple in the refrigerator. They both want the apple. Their negotiation is to discuss and argue why each should get the apple. They finally agree that they will flip a coin and the one who wins will get the apple. They flip the coin, and the brother wins and gets the apple. The sister loses and gets nothing.

Win-win results occur when all parties in the negotiation *get all, or at least part, of what they want and are happy with the results.* An example of this kind of negotiation is the ideal economic transaction where both parties exchange goods or services and they both are happier as a result. If you want to sell me a car for $9,000 and I, after inspecting the car, agree to pay you that amount, we have negotiated a win-win transaction. You are happier with the $9,000 than you were with the car, and I am happier with the car than the $9,000. We are both "winners."

Remember the brother and sister with the last apple in the house? If they used a win-win approach to their problem, they could either split the apple so that each would have half and both could be reasonably happy, they might agree that the brother would get the apple now but would give his sister his snack tomorrow, or the sister might get the apple and the brother could have a banana, which he likes just as much. There are many ways that the children could negotiate their problem if they start with the idea that they both should win.

It makes sense to try to negotiate in such a way that everyone can be a winner. It really isn't a difficult process, but it is difficult to break the habit of thinking that someone has to win and someone has to lose when we try to work out agreements. There are three steps to working out win-win agreements. They are:

1. ***Find out what the other person really wants.*** Very often it is difficult to know what the other person wants because he or she believes that a negotiator should hide what the real goal is.

2. ***Know what you really want.*** What is your goal? What are you willing to settle for? Do you possibly want to win just for the sake of winning?

3. ***Devise a way that you and the other person can both get what you want.*** This is where your creativity helps. The first difficult part is to avoid terms like "winner" and "loser"; however, if all parties agree that the goal of the negotiation is to have everyone win, there are usually many creative ways to bring this about. You CAN have an exciting, interesting, and rewarding experience finding a mutually-beneficial outcome to a problem. It becomes a challenge rather than a fight.

For another example of a win-win negotiation, suppose you are the parent of Janelle, who wants to go play with her friends, Teresa and Tamara; they live across a busy street from your house. Your goals are to keep your daughter safe and help her enjoy her friends. Janelle's goal is to play with her friends. You want to think of some way to make you both happy. What would you do? You could suggest that Janelle invite her friends to your house, but that might put them in danger when they crossed the street. You might be a bit more creative and suggest that Janelle could go play with Nicole or Taysia, who live on the same side of the street as you do, and there would not be any need to cross the dangerous street. If Janelle considers the idea of playing with Nicole or Taysia enjoyable, you have a win-win outcome.

Some characteristics of win-win negotiations are:

- The people involved try to defeat the problem at hand instead of each other.

- There is no human opponent. The opponent is the issue under discussion.

- Those involved see themselves working together for their mutual benefit.

- Honesty and trust play major roles. The traditional way of negotiating is to start the negotiations by overstating what you want, then conceding as the negotiations progress to what you are really willing to settle for. Win-win negotiating relies on everyone honestly working together from the beginning in a trusting relationship that is for the good of all involved.

- Win-win negotiations often involve compromise. When it becomes known what each person involved really wants, it is often necessary for individuals to give up part of what they want in order to gain part of what they want. For example, a husband who wants to go bowling one night a week knows that his wife will have to care for their children that evening by herself, so he offers to take the children on a different night so that his wife can go with friends to a movie.

- Win-win negotiations are built on empathy. Empathy is trying to "walk a mile in the other person's shoes," trying as best as you can to understand the problem from the other person's viewpoint.

Compromise does not mean a 50/50 split. If you watch many negotiations, you will note that a large percentage of them seem to assume that the final negotiation will be somewhere halfway between the initial positions. For example, if you and I pool our money and buy one turkey sandwich and an orange for lunch, we now need to decide or negotiate how we will divide our lunch. The first thing that would probably come into our minds would be to split the sandwich in half and to split the orange in half; however, if we talk about our wants, we might discover that you don't like oranges and I am a vegetarian. Now we decide to split the meal so that you get one slice of bread and the turkey and I get one slice of bread and the orange. We are both happy, but we didn't split the lunch exactly 50/50. If, for another example, we had to split a piece of cake between us, you might take the icing while I take the cake, and we are both quite happy. The idea here is to be creative in your ways of finding solutions to the problems you are negotiating. Every time you negotiate, you have the choice to work for agreements that result in

- Everybody losing,

- Some people winning,

- Some people losing,

- or everybody winning.

Choose to negotiate well.

QUESTIONS

1. Think of what you did yesterday. How many times did you try to come to an agreement (negotiate) with somebody? Did any of your negotiations result in lose-lose? Win-lose? Win-win?

2. Can you describe how lose-lose, win-lose, and win-win negotiations work? Use examples of each that would be clear and familiar to people your own age.

3. What would you say is the most important part of a win-win negotiation? Explain.

4. Why do you think that so many of us almost automatically start a negotiation with the intent of winning what we want but disregard what anyone else might want or need? Can you explain why we often want the other negotiator to lose?

5. Can you explain what is meant by trying to "defeat the problem rather than each other"?

ACTIVITIES

1. Create and write out an original situation involving people your age in which the negotiation results in a lose-lose situation for all involved. Share your situation with others in your group. Everyone should help each other to be sure that all the situations are the best possible examples of a lose-lose negotiation.

2. Create and write out an original situation involving people your age in which the negotiation results in a win-lose situation. Share your situation with the others in your group. Everyone should help each other to be sure that all the situations are the best possible examples of a win-lose negotiation.

3. Name all the contests, events, and other happenings you can think of that are win-lose situations. You have three minutes for this task, and the one with the most examples of win-lose situations wins. The others all lose.

4. Create and write out an original situation involving people your age in which the negotiation results in a win-win situation. Share your situation with the others in your group. Everyone should help each other to be sure that all the situations are the best possible examples of a win-win negotiation.

5. Produce a visual illustration (such as a drawing, cartoon, or picture) of situations that are clear examples of lose-lose,

win-lose, and win-win negotiations. Try to do all three if you can; however, it is fine if you can do only one or two. Display your creation(s) to the rest of the group. Can they tell which of the negotiations is being used in each creation? If they can't, can they suggest what would make the creation a clearer example of the negotiation?

6. Create a good example of each of the negotiation types out of the following classic cowboy movie: Tex and Pete are cowboys who are both in love with Marybelle, the waitress in the Dry Gulch Saloon. Marybelle isn't really interested in either one of them, but they each want the opportunity to court Marybelle. Can you create situations in which Tex and Pete negotiate for Marybelle using a lose-lose approach? A win-lose approach? A win-win approach? Write these as you would see them in some old, cheap cowboy movies and cartoons. Share your examples to get a laugh and check to see if your examples were clear to the others in your group.

7. Make a visual illustration of the three steps of a win-win negotiation.

8. Create two original examples of a compromise that is not a 50/50 split. Have them involve people who are about your age.

9. Create a situation with some member of your family or with a friend in which you have an issue that you must negotiate. Now exchange situations with someone else in your group. That person will describe one of the three negotiation

approaches using your characters in the situation you created. You will do the same with his or her written situation. When you have finished writing, take turns reading the negotiation approaches you devised. Discuss whether or not the approaches each of you devised were good examples. Continue exchanging papers and writing different approaches until both have completed all three approaches.

CHAPTER 19

Choose to Control Your Life

Who controls your life? Depending on your stage of development, you might answer that your life is controlled by your parents, teachers, spouse, boss, children, the government, your job, money, or even your pets. You might say that you are controlled by all of the above and perhaps add some more. The one you need to put as the number one controller of your life is *you*. The people and things outside you can influence you, but you make the ultimate decisions about your life. You always have a choice. A key to being productive and happy is to take advantage of the choices you have and deliberately control those choices.

For example, you have chosen to read this book. You can decide that today will be another interesting adventure in your life, or you can decide that it will be a rotten, boring, miserable, and thoroughly lousy day. You can elect to look for the good qualities in people, or you can elect to look for the worst qualities in people. You can choose to enjoy the present moment, or you can choose to think about your "unhappy past" or the "frightening future." You can decide that you are going to take deliberate control of your life, or you can decide that you will let people and events control you. You have the choice.

The major purpose of this book is to convince you that you should deliberately and consciously use terms like "choose" in both your thinking and speaking. Use these terms instead of those that give the control of your life to other people. Here are some examples of ways you might think to yourself or talk to others:

- I choose to...

- I allow myself to...

- I decide to…

- I select...

- I elect to...

- I accept...

You should think and talk using terms of this kind. You want to remind yourself constantly that you can and should be in control of your life.

If you think you are in control, you will be more likely to act as if you are in control. Remember that what you think about and expect is most likely to come about. When you say, "I choose," and, "I decide," you are also programming your mind to accept that you are in control. You always have this capability, but perhaps you just have not been in deliberate or conscious control. Now you can exert more control over your life because you will be making deliberate choices.

When you think and talk in terms like, "They made me do it," you are giving *them* power over your life. When you think and talk in terms like, "I decided to do it," you are giving yourself power over your life. You have the choice to do either.

You always have some choice, and that puts you in control, even if you only have control over a series of bad alternatives. For example, imagine that you are informed that you underpaid your income taxes last year and you must now pay a large sum of money plus the interest. In order to do this, you must either sell your beautiful car or move from your fantastic apartment to a less-than-fantastic apartment. You don't like the alternatives, but you do have choices. Your first possible choice is to not pay the taxes. This would not be a good choice because you could end up in jail. You can choose to sell your car and replace it with a cheaper one or you can move to a cheaper apartment. You still have some control over the situation, even if it is choosing the least undesirable alternative from among all undesirable alternatives.

If you are someone who feels that people, things, and events are controlling you and your life, you are under much more stress and strain than you need to be. Just thinking that you are not in control of something can make you feel uneasy and under stress. Just thinking that you are in control of a situation, and your life in general, can reduce your stress. When you think and speak in "I choose" terms, you can automatically alleviate some of the stress because you have decided that you will be in more control. When you were thinking, "They made me," or, "Mr. Smith wouldn't let me," or, "The government forced me to," you were bound to feel out of control. When you feel stressed, just thinking, "I choose to," can make you feel better. Try it.

If you are like most people, you will have to break habits of thinking and talking as if the rest of the world has control over your life. You will have to convince yourself that you can deliberately choose to take more responsibility for your life. You will have to consciously censor yourself to eliminate the kind of phrasing that gives control to other people, things, or events. Accept the fact that an unpleasant boss, a cold and rainy day, or unjust criticism can negatively influence you; however, they cannot control you unless you let them. You have to allow your boss to upset you. You have to decide that the rainy day will cause you to feel unhappy. You have to accept unjust criticism rather than openly choosing to reject it as untrue.

You always have some choices and, hence, some control. You must think of yourself as always having choices. You must consciously look for and identify those choices. You must decide which of those choices is the best and then act on it. You even have the choice to let other people make your decisions for you, but be prepared to live with the consequences of giving control of any part of your life to someone else.

- You are responsible for your life.

- You are in control of your life.

- You can **decide.** You can **select.** You can **pick.**

- You can **accept.** You can **elect.** You can **allow.**

- You can **choose.**

You can't control events, but you can control how you think about them.

QUESTIONS

1. Who is most in control of your life? Why?

2. Who should be most in control of your life? Why?

3. How can you be more in control of your life?

4. Do you want to be more in control of your life, or do you want others to make more of your decisions for you? Why?

5. Do you believe that you always have some choices? Explain your answer. Be sure to use examples to illustrate your answer.

6. Do you agree with the statement, "People who are less in control of their lives are more likely to experience stress than those people who are more in control of their lives"? Use examples, especially from your own life, to illustrate your answer.

ACTIVITIES

1. Explain how the idea that your taking responsibility for your choices relates to your being in control of your life. If possible, use a real example from your past or use a choice (or series of choices) you will need to make in the future to illustrate your explanation.

2. Your choices in life will determine *who* you will be and *what* you will become. What are some ideas and skills you should learn to increase the chances that those choices you will be making the rest of your life will be good ones? Share these ideas with the group and make a master list. This should provide a list of valuable ideas and skills you may want to begin learning to master.

3. Create a short story about a person who is in a situation in which he or she has choices but the choices are all bad alternatives. Use your imagination and perhaps make it humorous.

4. Explain how choosing to be in control of your life rather than choosing to let others control your life is related to the consequences with which you will have to live. Again, be sure to use examples to illustrate your answers.

5. What are some substitute ways of thinking about the following situations that would give you more control? For example, instead of saying, "My brother hurt my feelings

when he called me stupid," I should say, "I chose to allow my brother to hurt my feelings when he called me stupid."

 a) I get very upset when someone treats me with disrespect.

 b) I don't like to stop at stop signs.

 c) It makes me very angry when people use their mobile phones in restaurants where I am trying to have a quiet, restful meal.

6. Now create some situations of your own and share them with others in the group. See if they agree with you about ways in which you could rethink or rephrase the situation(s) to put yourself in more control.

CHAPTER 20

Never Ever Think of Yourself as a Failure

From now on, don't ever think of yourself as a failure. The word *failure* has a popular meaning that makes it seem bad if you don't succeed at something that you attempted to accomplish. Some people correlate not being successful at a task with not being successful as a person. In reality, you can fail at accomplishing a task or even several tasks and still be a very successful person.

Think of it this way. Pretend that someone gave you a big box full of keys and asked you to unlock a door. You look at the lock and the keys to determine which of the keys look like they fit the lock. Then you choose one of the keys and try it in the lock. The key does not fit.

At this point, you behave in one of two basic ways. One way is that you could think to yourself, "This key is one that does not fit the lock, so I'll put it aside so I won't waste my time trying it again. I have learned some valuable information about a key that does not work." You don't get upset, understanding that this is a trial and error process in which you will probably attempt several times unsuccessfully before you finally find the one key that fits.

Another way you could react to the same situation is to see the discovery that the key didn't work as a personal failure. You might think, "How could I be so stupid as to pick the wrong key?" or, "I must really be a dumb person to choose a key that didn't fit!" or, "I'm glad no one was watching me do something as embarrassing as that!" This is an example of turning a simple act like trying a key in a lock into a personal failure rather than seeing it as a little experiment with an outcome that was different from what you desired. **The real result of this experiment was information; not failure.** As the "experimenter," you have more information or knowledge than you did before the experiment; that certainly does not make you a failure.

How do you usually react to a situation where you were not as successful as you had hoped to be? Here are some ways *not* to think in situations of this kind.

- How could I be so stupid?
- I can't believe how dumb I am!
- I'm useless!
- I'm awful!
- I'll never be able to do that!
- I'll never try anything like that again!

Can you see how statements like these, even if you only think them to yourself, are making you think of yourself in negative ways? Can you see how you might take an event and then transfer that negativity to yourself? Such thoughts don't make sense when you think about it, but it happens to many people all the time whether they are parents, children, teachers, students, bosses, workers, coaches, players, or others. How can they and you avoid this self-defeating thinking? Try one or more of the following.

- *Don't use the word "failure."* Instead, use terms such as "result" (the result was not the one I would have preferred), "outcome" (the outcome was not what I expected), or "consequence" (I tried that and the consequence is less than I had hoped for). These terms are not negative; you are less likely to think of yourself as a failure.

- *Don't think about "failures."* Think of the negative result as being a postponement of what you wanted to accomplish.

- *Think about your life as a series of experiments.* Then the results of these experiments are simply information about whether the experiments work or don't work. Results don't judge the experimenter and you shouldn't either.

- *Think about what you used to call "failure" as just another kind of feedback from your environment.* Feedback is information you use in order to improve your life.

- *Instead of thinking "failure," think that this was a discovery of how not to do something.* Discoveries, in and of themselves, are rarely considered in a negative light.

- *If you do make some kind of a mistake, simply say to yourself, "That isn't the way I usually behave," or, "That just isn't like me."* Then resolve not to make the same error again.

- *If you must judge something, judge the event and not yourself. The event was undesirable, but you are still an interesting, bright, and wonderful person.*

- *Rather than thinking in terms of "failure," you might think in terms of "not meeting your expectations."* For example, you might have expected to win first place in a competition, but you came in second. That does not mean you are a failure. In fact, it is fantastic because only one thing was between you and the accomplishment of your greatest expectation.

- *Recognize what you used to call a "failure" as a learning event.* If the result didn't please you, what can you do differently next time? Perhaps you need to be better prepared. Maybe you overlooked something that you can include next time. Some people try to look at all events in their lives as learning experiences whether the event was positive or negative.

- *Don't compare yourself to others.* A lot of people who think who they are failures believe so because they compare themselves to other people. If you think about it, there is no reason why you should compare yourself to other people. This is because you can always find someone who is richer than you, who can run faster, has better "luck," or has a nicer house. Likewise, you can always find someone who is poorer, who doesn't have the legs to run, who has terrible "luck," and who doesn't have a home. It doesn't make you a failure when you compare yourself to others more fortunate any more than it makes you a success when you compare yourself to those who are less fortunate. There is nobody else in the world like you. You are unique. Just think of yourself as a unique and responsible person who doesn't get involved in comparing yourself with anybody else.

- *Don't worry about your life experiments that don't turn out as you expected.* Learn from these "temporary postponements of your progress" and then forget them. Don't waste your valuable energy and time mentally recycling what went wrong and what you should have done. You can't go back to change it, so why even think about it anymore? Don't waste your present by reliving your negative past.

Perhaps there is one true "failure." The one real failure is not attempting something that you really want to do. If you try something and it doesn't work out as you expected, that is feedback, but if you don't try something at all, that is failure. *Never give up a dream because of the fear of negative feedback.*

From now on, you will not have "failures." You will often get negative feedback. You will have many learning experiences. You will find many ways not to do things. You will do some things that are uncharacteristic of your behavior. You

187

will find that events in your life can be interpreted as negative or they can be interpreted as positive.

No matter how successful you become, you will have some temporary setbacks. You will find that there is no "failure" in the world. The world only gives feedback about your behavior.

Your thinking will determine whether you are a "failure" or an experimenter who is a little bit wiser.

QUESTIONS

1. How do you define the word failure? Is your definition more like simply getting feedback or is it more like personally being a failure?

2. How do you react to the idea of "thinking of your life as a series of experiments and that sometimes your experiments give you outcomes that are positive and sometimes negative"? Does that make sense to you? Why or why not?

3. Do you ever compare yourself to others? Do you usually compare yourself to people whom you perceive to have less than you and who seem less fortunate, or do you usually compare yourself to people whom you perceive to have more than you and who seem more fortunate? How does it feel? Is there a lesson to be learned?

4. What if you never compared yourself to anyone? Do you think you would be any happier or less happy? Does comparing yourself to others change you as a person in any way?

5. Have you ever given up a dream or not tried something because you were afraid of negative feedback (failure)? What would have been a better way for you to have dealt with that situation?

ACTIVITIES

1. Think of some times in your life in which you perceived that you failed at something. Did you take that as your being a personal failure, or did you take it more as feedback that you could use to improve? Explain.

2. Create a situation in which a fictional person is not as successful as he or she had hoped to be. Now write one ending to the situation in which the person takes the temporary disappointment as a personal failure. Next, write an ending that shows how the person uses the failure or disappointment as feedback that can be used to improve him or herself. If you are in a group, share your two stories with others and have them share their stories with you. Do you all agree that the stories are good examples of personal-failure thinking and feedback-to-use thinking?

3. You have decided that you will not use the word failure again. What word would you use? Why? Use a dictionary or a thesaurus to find words that do not convey the notion of personal failure or something of which to be ashamed. Share your word(s) with others and find out what they have chosen.

4. Can you explain how using failures as feedback might be analogous to driving a car or flying a plane? What other analogies can you think of that could help explain the usefulness of this failure-as-feedback idea?

5. Can you think of times in your life in which you perceived that you failed at something and then kept thinking about it over and over? Maybe you thought about it when you were in bed at night and you couldn't sleep because you kept reliving your negative experience. What was the situation? Did it help you in any way to keep replaying your temporary inconvenience over and over? What would be better ways to deal with these situations rather than going over the failure in your mind?

6. Write a short paragraph that describes how you will behave the next time you are not as successful as you had hoped to be. Create a specific situation that could possibly happen. What will you say to yourself? What will you do? How might you describe the situation to someone else?

CHAPTER 21

You Can't Just Escape from Something Without Ending Up Somewhere Else

Children run away from home. Spouses separate from spouses. Workers resign from jobs. Students quit school. These are just a few of the ways that people escape from situations they don't like. The child doesn't like to clean his room, so he runs away. The spouse doesn't like some of the other spouse's habits, so she leaves. The worker doesn't like the demands of his boss, so he quits his job. The student doesn't like the rules in the school, so she leaves. It is natural for people to want to avoid negative experiences; however, you need to remember the old saying, "Out of the frying pan and into the fire," to keep in mind that escaping from something doesn't guarantee that your new situation will be better.

The child who runs away from home often finds a hostile world that has restrictions far more limiting than those of his parents. A person might get divorced but finds that life alone or with a new mate is even less desirable. The person who quits his job because of an undesirable boss might find that his next boss is a modern version of Attila the Hun. The student who quits school often finds the world outside of school to be much more hostile than inside school. How can you guard against escaping from a bad situation only to get yourself into a worse one?

You might consider an approach to making changes in your life in which you would always think in terms of moving *toward* something rather than moving *away* from something. In other words, your focus in making a change is on the place you want to be rather than on where you don't want to be. For example, if you find that you are in a job that you don't find fulfilling, even though you have tried to make it that way, you should then focus on finding a new position that offers the kind of work you would find rewarding. You think of the characteristics of a new job that would meet your desires for feeling fulfilled, being stimulated, providing human needs, and more. In this way, your energy is aimed at where you want to be and what you want to do to improve your life.

When you think about an anticipated change as being toward a positive goal, you can be conscious of where you are going in comparison to where you are now. This will help you to answer the "why" question. You can assess whether the change is worth it or not before you act. If you are only thinking about running away from something, you have no basis for comparison between where you are now and where you will be if you change.

For example, imagine that you don't like the city in which you are living. You wouldn't just move out of your city to get away from it. You would look at other cities for the qualities you desire and compare them to the city in which you now live. You would stay or move based on this evaluation. You would never consider moving from the city you know you don't like without first investigating where you might be happy and being reasonably certain that you would enjoy it more.

Many of our major, as well as minor, decisions, however, are made from the "just let me escape" approach without consideration of where the escape will lead. *You can't just escape from something without ending up somewhere else.* It is the "somewhere else" that you want to keep foremost in your mind.

Life is full of less-than-perfect situations. If you run from less-than-perfect situations, you will be running away from something all the time.

You must give at least as much time to planning where you want to be as to planning where you don't want to be.

QUESTIONS

1. What does the title of this chapter mean to you?

2. What meaning or meanings does the chapter have for you?

3. Have you ever escaped from something only to find out that you were worse off after you escaped? What happened?

4. What does it mean to you when the chapter states that you should ask "why" before you take an action?

5. Do you know of anyone who seems to have acted without first asking "why"? What happened? Can you describe the situation and the consequences?

6. Is there any idea in the chapter with which you disagree? Why?

7. Do you think this chapter gives good advice or not? Why?

8. What would you say are the key ingredients to making a good decision about escaping from what you perceive to be a bad situation?

ACTIVITIES

1. Describe a story about a person your age who makes a decision to escape from what he or she thinks is a bad situation but ends up in an even worse situation.

2. Describe a story about a person your age who makes a decision to escape from a bad situation and ends up in a much better situation.

3. Illustrate (by a drawing, painting, poetry, or some other artistic way) one of the ideas in this chapter that you think is important.

4. Describe the way you would explain the idea of moving *toward* something rather than moving *away* from something to a young child.

CHAPTER 22

The Real Heroes

The real heroes are around us every day, but we don't usually see them, and we very seldom acknowledge them. Real heroes differ from the heroes who are depicted on television and in the movies. Television heroes are usually people who save someone's life in a daring, but often unthinking, split-second situation. For example, a man who is walking down the street sees a burning house, runs into it, and saves the life of a child. This is a heroic act, but it is done in only a few seconds with little or no deliberation. The man does not weigh the pros and cons of going into the burning house. He does not have time to determine his odds of getting out of the house alive. If he had time to consider all of the consequences, he might not even do it. He reacts almost instinctively and, if he is successful, he is a hero. He risks his life but for only a few seconds or minutes. Everyone has seen or heard of this kind of brave act. This is heroism, but it is just one kind of heroism.

Perhaps the real heroes are those people who, day in and day out, over long periods of time, act in brave and unselfish ways. There are real heroes who quietly and painfully overcome personal hardships unimagined by most of us. There are other real heroes who help other people over long periods of time without ever being recognized for their contributions. Real heroes show the best in human behavior without the expectation of rewards or recognition. Real heroes determine that they will make a difference even if making that difference entails some personal risk. These real heroes do what they know is right even when others, perhaps a large majority of others, disagree with them and try to get them to conform.

Who are some of these real heroes?

- Real heroes are those people who have lost their limbs but who go to work in their wheelchairs every day, are always on time, and perform as well as, or better than, their colleagues.

- Real courage is shown by people who are disfigured but who go out every day into a world that worships beauty.

- Real heroes are parents who dedicate themselves to a lifetime of caring for their child who is profoundly mentally challenged. They choose this path out of love and responsibility rather than taking the easier path of giving the child to a social agency.

- Many parents and grandparents quietly help their grown children or grandchildren in times of crisis even when it means that they decrease their lifestyle, endure hardships, or use some of their life savings. This kind of heroism often goes unrecognized and unappreciated.

- Heroism occurs when the politician votes for a bill because it is in the best interest of the general welfare even though it is unpopular with constituents or major campaign contributors.

• Some real modern heroes are those parents (usually mothers) who dedicate themselves to the awesome responsibilities of raising their children when society generally doesn't recognize or reward this dedication. They understand the importance of bringing up their children, and they do it diligently and with love while being constantly told that real fulfillment can only be found outside the home.

• Perhaps real heroes could also be included among those divorced fathers who continue to make the payments for the support of their children even though they see other fathers not meeting their responsibilities and getting away with it.

• Real heroism is the aging person who, despite chronic pain, is always first to greet you with a smile, an encouraging word, and an observation of what a wonderful day it is to be alive.

• Real heroes are those people who somehow are able to overcome generations of family poverty and reliance on government assistance to become self-reliant. It takes a sustained sense of purpose, tremendous strength, drive, and determination to overcome all of the factors that keep saying " conform to the status quo and accept what has been as what always will be."

• Heroism is standing up for what you believe is right even though there is a good chance that you could be hurt by it.

• Perhaps heroism also is doing what you know is right even when no one else is looking or when everyone else is doing the wrong thing.

Perhaps you know some of these real heroes. Maybe you can identify others who are equally deserving of being defined as real heroes. If you know some unsung heroes, be sure to recognize them, reward them, and otherwise let them know that they are appreciated. Thank them and salute them.

Perhaps you are one of these real heroes. If you are, I want to thank you and salute you.

QUESTIONS

1. What do you believe it takes to be a real hero? That is, what criteria or qualities do you use to judge whether or not a person is a hero?

2. Can you add any heroes to the list in this chapter?

3. Can you think of someone who fits at least five of the hero categories described in this chapter?

4. Do you see a relationship between heroism and responsibility? Can you describe that relationship? Use examples.

5. Do you know anyone your own age who could be classified as a hero in some way? Could you be classified as a hero in some way?

6. What might you do to become a hero by the definition used in this chapter? Visualize yourself as being that hero.

7. Are there people who are sometimes classified as heroes who you think do not deserve that title? Who are those people? Why do you think they should not be thought of as heroes?

8. Many times people who are seen as heroes are also seen as role models. That is, they are viewed as people to admire and emulate (someone to be like). Do you have any heroes like that? Do you want to be like that person or do they have

some qualities you would like to have and other qualities that you would rather not have?

9. What do you think is the best name or description of someone who is the opposite of a hero?

10. What are some other words that mean the same as "hero"?

11. What do you think would be the most heroic thing someone could do?

12. If you could be remembered for doing something heroic, what would you like it to be?

ACTIVITIES

1. Do you think there are different kinds of heroism? What might they be? Share your ideas with others and see if you can make a master list of different kinds of heroism. Is one kind of heroism "better" than the rest? Have everyone in your group make a list of people he or she perceives as heroes. What qualities do they have? What is it that is most admirable about each one? Do some or all of them also have some qualities that you don't admire? Are there some qualities that you admire but that other people don't admire? Why do you suppose that these differences exist?

2. Do you know of someone who fits the "real hero" definition of someone who, over long periods of time, acts in brave and unselfish ways even though he or she gets little or no formal recognition? If you know of such a person or persons, why don't you or your group recognize those people in some way? Let them know how much they are appreciated and how much you respect their strength. Be especially aware of family members whom you might have taken for granted and therefore overlooked their heroism.

3. Do you disagree with any of the descriptions of heroes in this chapter? If so, why?

4. Do you know any specific real heroes from the following list? Name him or her and be prepared to give your reasons why.

    *   A parent or guardian

    *   A teacher

    *   A professional athlete

- A brother or sister

- A relative

- A person from history

- Someone who lives in your neighborhood

- Someone you have known in school

- A politician

- Someone who has a disability

- A movie star

- A music video star

- Someone who is more than 60 years old

- Someone else not mentioned above

5. Using the preceding list, name the five areas from which your heroes are most likely to come. Why did you pick them? What five areas would represent the areas from which your heroes would be least likely to come? Explain.

CHAPTER 23

Strategies to Use, Prevent, Reduce, and Control Stress

It is natural to have stress. When we encounter a situation that we perceive as both undesirable and out of our control, we often refer to it as stressful. In order to gain some kind of control over the situation, our bodies make rapid adjustments that allow us to deal with the situation physically, much like our ancient ancestors did. That is, we get a series of physical "boosts" to better help us either avoid the situation (run away from it as fast as we can) or meet it head-on (physically attack the threat or defend ourselves) as described in the familiar phrase, "fight or flight."

For example, the caveman who met a giant bear on the path had little choice other than to run away from the bear or to fight it. There was little room for negotiation as we know it today. The only negotiation was the most rapid as possible *negotiation* of the path back to the safety of his cave. If retreat was not a good alternative, he would have to fight the bear.

In order to provide optimal survival possibilities to the caveman, his body sped up his metabolic rate, heart rate, and breathing rate; it tensed his muscles, caused arteries to spasm, and increased platelet clumping ability. These were adaptations that gave the caveman quick energy, provided him with a denser shield of muscle, and decreased the chances of profuse bleeding.

Our ancestors, who survived many crises of this kind, evolved physiological systems that performed these changes especially well. Those who had bodies that did not make these quick adaptations did not survive. We inherited physiological systems that are quite efficient in making adjustments in crisis situations. Lucky us!

Times have changed, however. Our caveman ancestors spent most of their days concerned with the most basic elements of living. Most of their lives were spent in the routines of looking for food and resting. Once in a while they would encounter dangers that required their run or fight mechanism to be activated. If they survived the crisis, the danger would pass and the body would return to normal. That is, the metabolic, breathing, and heart rates would slow down; the muscles and arteries would relax; and platelets would not clump as easily. In other words, the caveman had stress, but it was not very frequent, it was over rather quickly, and afterward the caveman went back to a relatively stress-free life.

Today, the run or fight defense mechanism is still a part of human physiology, but times have changed. This survival mechanism may now be working against many of us. Many of us find large amounts of stress in our everyday world because we consistently interpret parts of our lives as negative and believe we have no control over them. Some of us interpret nearly everything throughout our day as being negative and out of our control. Our nervous systems react to these everyday situations in essentially the same way as the caveman's nervous system reacted to the chance meeting of a dangerous animal.

We normally do not behave the same way to our stress on the highway (or other stressful situations), however, as the caveman did when he encountered danger on the path. He ran away or stayed and fought the ancient enemy on the trail. Today you usually do not run away from or fight the office bully who constantly makes your life miserable. Even though your breathing speeds up, blood pressure rises, heart rate increases, muscles tense, general metabolism rises, arteries spasm, and your platelets are more likely to clump, you can't utilize these crisis mechanisms and battle or escape in the same ways your ancestors did. The modern battle or escape is much less physical and much less likely to be quickly resolved.

Modern life with its tight schedules, multiple roles, rapid changes, less family stability, constant negative news, emphasis on competition, among other things, contains many situations that can be interpreted as negative and out of our control. We also seem to have more situations that do not have closure and just seem to nag at us constantly. These are situations that can lead us to interpret large parts of our lives as stressful over long periods of time. With the perceived stress comes the automatic crisis mechanisms described earlier. This means, however, that the increased breathing, raised blood pressure, increased metabolism, increased heart rate, tensed muscles, arterial spasms, and platelet clumping are activated many more times and continue over a much longer period of time than they were designed for originally.

The problem is made greater because the body is responding to an anticipated physical reaction to the stress rather than to the kinds of responses that we are socially and legally obligated to make to today's stresses. Rather than having a quick response to an immediate and short-lived physical situation, the body changes described above can become long-term contributors to hypertension (high blood pressure), backaches, rashes, upset stomach, inability to sleep or relax, short temper, muscle spasms, sore muscles, headaches, and higher probabilities of heart attacks and strokes. Thus, this fantastic short-term survival mechanism can become a long-term threat to our survival if we don't understand it or don't use it properly. It is helpful to keep the following information about stress in mind.

- ***Stress is in your head.*** You create or manufacture your stress by the ways in which you think. The world doesn't have stress in it that you can touch, smell, see, or taste. For example, your boss doesn't make you stressed. He or she can only do things such as finding fault with your work or giving unclear directions. You then interpret these actions in such a way as to make you feel stressed. "My boss is driving me crazy because he never says anything good about my work." You could just as well think, "It's too bad that my boss doesn't praise me for all the good work that I do, but I know how valuable I am, and I can live with that." In the same way, unclear directions can be strains on you or they can be opportunities for you to have more creativity in your work. You can't have stress without your being at least partially responsible because you have to make that interpretation of stress by the way you think.

• *Everything is a possible source of stress.* How you interpret any given situation determines how stressful it will be. Travel to a foreign country can be seen as a great opportunity to meet different and interesting people, or it can be seen as a fearful confrontation with unfamiliar and probably criminal people. A small, non-poisonous snake can be seen as an attractive creature that has graceful movements, or it can be seen as a frightful reptile from which you must run. If you allow yourself to be prone to stress, you can find some stress in anything.

• *How you interpret any situation depends on your prior learning and your belief system.* For example, your parents and friends have taught you that a certain ethnic group is *bad*. You later become lost and find yourself in a neighborhood of this ethnic group and are quite frightened. Your belief system has a tremendous impact on whether or not you view a given situation as one that involves stress. If you have been taught that the world is essentially a bad place, you are more likely to interpret events and people as *bad* and, hence, more stressful to you.

• *Some kinds of tension can be good for you.* When you find yourself in a real crisis situation

210

that requires a fight or flight type of physical response (e.g., you are attacked by a mugger, you must escape from a burning building, you want to free someone who is pinned under a pile of rubble, etc.), you want the physiological reaction that you inherited from your caveman ancestors to be activated to give you the best chance possible of survival.

You may also want to have a little normal, but well-controlled, tension to keep you on your toes when you are preparing for a game, speech, or other type of performance. When you feel that you have control of the situation, the task is interesting, and that what you are doing is valuable, you will not trigger the flight or fight mechanism. You might allow yourself a few butterflies in the stomach or anticipatory tension, however, before the tennis match, your speech, or the play in which you are an actor. Keep your tensions and stresses short-term and controlled. In fact, this is a good habit to follow any time you encounter a bad situation. View it as short-lived and within your control.

Control is perhaps the key factor in stressful situations. In most cases, the more you feel you are in control, the less the probability of stress. Conversely, the less you feel in control, the more likely you are to experience stress. For example, you are less likely to be stressed if you are driving your car down a dangerous highway than if you are a passenger in an airplane, which is proven to be a much safer means of transportation. Having control gives you more of a sense of security, which is the antithesis of stress.

If stress is brought about primarily by the way you think about things that happen to you, and you can control your thoughts, then you can control your stress by how you think. In other words, if you can learn skills to control your thinking, you can increase your control over your stress. The best example of this is a positive attitude. If you always look for the positive in any situation, you will lessen the probability of stress because stress thrives on the negative. Any time you feel the symptoms of stress, do a quick check on your thinking about that situation because the situation isn't causing the stress—your thinking is.

Ways to Prevent and Reduce Stress

Each of the following represents a way in which you can prevent or reduce your stress. Note how your thoughts about situations, and specifically taking control of those situations, are keys to both preventing and reducing your stress.

Accept the fact that it is natural to have stressful situations in your life while understanding that you have control over how you react to them. You know you have headaches because you have over-committed yourself. Now you are going to concentrate on the most important tasks and accept the fact that you will have to let the others slide for a while. If that doesn't work, you will find someone to complete some of the lesser tasks.

Avoid situations that have a high potential for being stressful. When possible, avoid the negative colleague, don't stay in an unfulfilling job, ignore your obnoxious neighbor, transfer to a different department if your department has an unreasonable boss, or get rid of the car that keeps breaking down. You must carefully consider the long-term consequences of avoiding any situation, however. This is not to be seen only as avoiding a bad situation. It must be primarily moving toward a better situation. You do not want to avoid a bad situation only to get yourself into a horrible situation.

Always look for the positive in situations. Your plate is half full, not half empty. You might lose some money, but you still have your health. You didn't fail; you just learned another way *not* to do something. You celebrate the deceased person's life and you move on; you don't perpetually mourn his or her death.

Accept responsibility for any stress you experience. If your stress cannot exist without your thinking, it has to be coming from inside you. You are responsible, in large part, for your stress. It is not realistic for you to blame your stress on something outside you. Whether the situation is a legitimately stressful one or whether it isn't, you are responsible for that interpretation. This is why you need to be careful in the way you interpret situations.

Have some goals on which to focus your energy. Stress can be the result of aimless activity. You do a lot of work, but never seem to be getting anywhere. Other people may seem to be passing you by—even though you are working as hard as or harder than they are. You can become increasingly frustrated as you burn up energy going in circles because you are not sure of a specific direction in which you want to go.

If you have too many goals, prioritize them and work on the most important one(s). Stress can be the result of too many goals. If you believe you have to accomplish more things than time permits, you are putting yourself into a classic modern stressful situation. When you find this is happening to you, you can get control of the situation by prioritizing your goals so you can concentrate your efforts on your most important goal or goals. Thus, you can use your finite time and energy in more productive ways. It is usually good mental health to concentrate on a priority task, finish it, feel the satisfaction, and then go on to the next highest priority. One simple way to lessen stressful situations is to decline taking on more tasks in the first place.

Don't worry about the past. One of the most non-productive activities you can do is to think about what you should have done. The past is gone. You certainly should use your experiences as learning situations, but don't dwell on decisions or actions that didn't work out the way you would have preferred. You can't go back and do what you should have done, and you can't go back and *not* do what you shouldn't have done. If you feel you must mentally revisit the past, think about events and people who make you feel good about your accomplishments and your abilities.

213

Celebrate improvement rather than expect perfection. We can all improve, but no one can be perfect. If you only accept perfection as your standard, you automatically set yourself up for stress because you have set an impossible criterion. You can be happier, but you probably will never be completely happy, at least not for long. Many people avoid this kind of stress by striving to get a little better and rewarding themselves for that improvement.

Expect success but accept some setbacks as natural. Setbacks are normal, natural consequences of trying. Any time you undertake something, there is the possibility that it might not develop as you had anticipated. Even though you visualize and expect success, plan, and work hard, you probably will have some setbacks. You can overcome these setbacks by having a clear goal and viewing "failures" as temporary inconveniences that you can overcome. You do not think of the setback as being unsuccessful because you do not see it as a permanent failure out of your control. It is rather seen as a temporary slowing of your progress. You do not even use the word "failure" in your thinking. You know that the only real failure is never to try.

Work smarter, not harder. Much frustration and distress is caused when you try to solve problems by continuing to repeat the same action that doesn't work rather than taking the time to find new perspectives and new approaches. This is not meant to discourage you from working hard. It does mean that if trying to beat down the brick wall with a hammer doesn't work, maybe it is time to see if there is a way around, under, or over it. Working smarter is also a lot more interesting and exciting than just working harder.

Accept responsibility for the use of your time. Don't say, "I didn't have the time." That kind of thinking puts you out of control of your time and puts you in a potentially stressful situation. Say, "I did not take the time." This puts you mentally in control and makes it obvious that you are using your time doing what you choose as being most important at that time. When you deliberately prioritize the use of your time, you are controlling your time rather than having time control you.

Think in specifics. We often refer to "they," "the government," "the administration," "the bureaucracy," and other entities as being sources of our stress. These vague forces in our minds are difficult or impossible to control. This leads to great frustration because you can't talk to "them." "They" can't help you solve your problem. Not getting closure to a problem can be a major source of potential stress. You have to find Mr. Jones, the person who made the decision that is causing you problems. Mr. Jones can talk to you and discuss your problem with you. Now you have some input and control over the situation and the stress is reduced or avoided. A specific caused the situation; a generality didn't. A specific is needed to change it.

Be "in control" and choose, even when your choices are all undesirable ones. You always have a choice of doing something or not doing something; however, you might catch yourself saying something like, "He made me do it," which indicates that you do not see yourself in control of that part of your life. You might be better off saying, "I choose to do it because the bad consequence of *not* doing it is worse than the bad consequence of doing it." In this case, you have taken control and have made a rational choice among undesirable alternatives rather than just accepting an inevitable negative fate that was beyond your control. Thinking of yourself as in control not only can reduce your stress, but it can also better describe the reality that you always have some choices in every situation.

Be careful how you describe yourself when you have less control than you would like. You may have referred to yourself as stressed-out, sick and tired of something, at the end of your rope, or not being able to take it anymore. Such similar terms indicate that you had little or no control at that point or that you were about to lose control if one more negative thing happened. You need to substitute phrases such as *temporarily inconvenient, undesirable but controllable*, and *unfortunate but getting better* in your self-talk as well as in your conversations with others. These terms indicate that you retain control of your life and will not interpret situations in such a way; thinking of yourself being stressed actually causes stress.

Don't allow yourself to get upset over rumors, hearsay, and other unreliable data. For example, some employees get very upset when they hear the rumor that their company will be closed. Finally, after some days have gone by, one of them talks to management and finds out that there is no truth to the rumor. The distress they caused themselves was completely unwarranted and would not have happened if they had gotten the facts rather than accepting the rumors without question. You can reduce stressful situations by dealing with facts and seeking reality.

Accept the fact that there are things over which you have no control. You may become upset about a plane crash in England, even though it does not involve you in any direct way. You feel further frustrated because there is nothing you can do about it. Note how this potential stress is increased by the mass media, which is full of bad news over which you have no control. Watching, listening, and reading this constant flow of negativity can lead to stress, frustration, and cynicism. You could reduce your input of this negativity by ignoring the news; however many of us want to be informed and, hence, will continue to consume it. In that case, either do something to rectify the negative situation or accept the fact that it is an event over which you have no control. Make a conscious decision and move on.

Be assertive when you feel you have been wronged. What do you do if a merchant sells you an inferior product? Do you keep the product, get angry, hate the merchant, and build up your stress? Or do you politely, but firmly, assert your right to a replacement or refund? Being assertive is nothing more than diplomatically standing up for what you think is right. This is controlling your life and reducing the potential for stress.

Cultivate friends who are positive in their outlooks. Negative people can subtly influence your thinking to negative thoughts if you allow them to do so. Avoid those people who talk negatively about others, spread spiteful gossip, see the worst in every situation, and generally leave you feeling worse than before you met them. Try to surround yourself with positive people who enjoy life, find the best in people and situations, have a good sense of humor, and who make you feel good about being alive.

Confront undesirable situations as soon as you can. A sure way to increase your stress is to put off dealing with an undesirable situation. While you are procrastinating, you are likely to imagine the situation to be much worse than it really is. Not doing something that you know you need to do is almost always much worse than doing what you need to do. Procrastination and stress go hand in hand. Aren't you always under more stress during the time that you are procrastinating than when you are actually dealing with it?

Don't expect reciprocity. Some people become upset, frustrated, or angry because they give a gift or do a favor and do not get their favor returned. Give a gift or favor for the joy of giving and the happiness of the person to whom the gift is given without any expectation of anything in return.

Don't make elephant droppings out of flyspecks. Some of us are quite good at taking a small incident and thinking it into a major disaster. As a disaster it adds to our stress but in the reality of being a small incident, it is only an inconvenience. An accidental small scratch on someone's new car can grow into a fight where injury or death can result. Our thinking manufactures many catastrophes from small, often insignificant happenings.

Defuse stress with humor. Laughing at yourself or at the situation can often be the quickest way to break tension and other forms of stress. Look for the ridiculous in a situation. Joking about a bad situation makes it less likely that you will think of it in catastrophic terms. This defuses the caveman response of stress. Sometimes a simple smile can defuse stress. Try it. Smile and say, "I feel so stressed!"

Reduce or discontinue stimulants. Most people find they are less tense when they reduce or stop their use of caffeine (usually coffee, regular tea, and cola drinks), nicotine, and sugars. Again, moderation is important.

If you feel stressed, take a mental trip to a favorite spot or mentally do something that is especially enjoyable to you. Substitute your feelings of tension and stress with relaxing thoughts about a favorite place or activity such as the seashore, forest, cathedral, sailing, playing ball, or another activity. Your alternatives are as unlimited as your imagination.

If you feel stressed, do some relaxation exercises. There are many relaxation exercises. One of the most popular exercises is to begin at your feet and tense your muscles then relax them as you work your way up your body until your whole body is relaxed. Meditation is proven to be a simple and effective way to reduce stress and to refresh oneself. Try several to find some that work for you.

Regular exercise is a good way both to prevent and treat stress. Walking, jogging, swimming, biking, and other exercises in which the heart rate is moderately elevated over a relatively long time are valuable not only in dealing with stress, but are also excellent for strengthening the cardiovascular system. Any exercise is better than none, but aerobic exercise for at least 30 minutes, four or five times a week is generally accepted as a good compromise between time expended and benefits derived.

Make a decision and then enjoy it. Many people have the habit of making a decision and then, almost immediately, starting to second-guess themselves. Second-guessing and doubting build unnecessary stress. If you buy a white car, enjoy it and don't think that you should have purchased the red one. You should enjoy the benefits resulting from your well-researched decisions rather than increasing your turmoil by continuing to debate alternatives even after the decisions have been made.

Recognize the fact that almost any change will bring a greater-than-normal potential for stress. Changes in your life, even the ones that are for the most part positive, can cause anxiety and stress if you allow them to do so. Changes involve the uneasiness of breaking comfortable patterns and the anxiety of entering the unknown. It is natural to have some stressful feelings when you enter the unfamiliar, so accept them as natural and look for the stimulation and excitement of exploring new territory. Change is a chance to grow, and you can't grow without changing. Change does not have to be stressful; whether or not it is stressful is primarily because of your thinking.

How important is it? One way to help yourself keep perspective is to make a sign of the following two rules and keep it in a place where you will see it often.

Rule #1: Don't sweat the small stuff.

Rule #2: Maybe it's all small stuff.

Think of problems as being opportunities. Many people reduce their tension and stress by thinking of negative situations as being opportunities to see new prospects, creatively solve problems, and develop positives out of negatives. For example, the problem of the theft of a tool you use in your work could become an opportunity to invent a new tool.

Accept the fact that not everyone will like you or what you do. You can reduce a lot of potential stress from your life if you keep in mind that you will never be able to please everybody. Human beings come with too many varieties of values and outlooks for you to expect to please them all. Trying to please all of one's potential critics is a sure way to increase stress.

Do your best and feel good about it, even if it isn't perfect. Set high standards for yourself, but make sure that those standards are realistic. Being a perfectionist is not realistic.

No one is perfect, at least not for long; however, it is realistic to put your best effort into achieving your goals. If you do your best at something, you can be satisfied with yourself. You have used as much of your potential as you know how and you, or anyone else, cannot expect any more than that. If something is not worth your best effort, then it probably isn't worth doing in the first place.

Understand that all choices involve some kind of trade-off. Every time you choose one thing, you have to give up something else. If you don't understand this, you can be an unhappy and tense person who is always looking for the 100% fail-proof, completely correct answer or decision. Since there isn't such a perfect guarantee, you are setting yourself up for an endless, fruitless, and frustrating search. Analyze the trade-offs in any decision-making situation, make your choice, accept the things you have to forego, and then enjoy your choice.

Accept the fact that people are not likely to change into the way you want them to be. One of the situations with the highest potential to cause you stress occurs when you experience the frustrations of trying to get someone else to change to meet your expectations. Others change when they see the need—not when you see the need. Attempting to force someone to change without their desire to do so can become especially stressful to all involved.

Get rid of "clutter" in your life. Messy houses, garages, closets, offices, desks, cars, and so on are potential sources of stress because they represent constant reminders of things that you need to get done. They nag at you whenever you encounter them. Tidy up the physical things in your life and see if you don't feel more relaxed because you automatically tidied up your mind in the process.

Complete your unfinished relationship business. This includes relationships or any dealings with people or organizations that are now at an uncomfortable stage. Apologize to your sister for the angry things you said. Send a thank you letter to someone who did you a favor. Send a note of praise to the principal or teacher who is doing such a great job with your child. You might think of this as cleaning up your relationships much the same way that you would clean up the physical clutter in your life. As you overcome procrastination and bring closure to this unfinished human relationship business, you will reduce much potential stress.

Be consistent in your beliefs and actions. If you choose to behave in ways that are inconsistent with what you profess to be your belief system, you are creating situations with high potential for stress. To do something that you know is wrong creates a form of self-dishonesty, or hypocrisy. Any sane person will feel tension when they knowingly behave in ways that are incongruent with their professed belief system. Actually, you behave consistently with what you believe is best for you at that time. What you profess to be your belief might be different.

Determine when to stop. You can create a potentially stressful situation when you don't think about when you are overdoing something. Writing term papers creates stressful situations for students when they continue going to the library "just one more time" for more sources when they know they need to be sitting down and writing. In the same way, some of us will spend hours shopping for an item to find it a few cents cheaper when we could pay a fair amount after pricing the item at just two or three stores. Consider setting realistic limits as guides for knowing when to stop. Some people, for example, will set a dollar amount below which they will not comparison shop. They will only comparison shop for the more expensive items above that limit. This saves them a lot of time and hassle. What would your dollar amount be below which you would not comparison shop?

Choose a career you love. When you choose your vocation, choose something that you really love to do if you possibly can. Income from the position certainly should be considered, but the happiest and most stress-resistant people are those who really love their work. It seems that it is easier to adjust one's economic lifestyle than it is to find work that is interesting, exciting, and fulfilling. When you find a vocation to which you can be highly committed, you probably will do it well and make a reasonable living as a result. But there is no guarantee.

Don't compare yourself to others. It is very easy to create a potentially stressful situation when you compare yourself to those who seem to be the richest, most famous, most talented, and happiest people. If you must compare yourself, compare yourself to someone who has less than you. It is probably best not to compare yourself to anyone, however. What purpose does it serve? Be proud of who you are and what you contribute.

Add variety to your life. Stress can occur when you have been doing the same thing for too long. This form of burnout usually is indicated by boredom and a loss of the feeling of challenge. Adding variety and change in your life can lessen the sameness often described as being in a rut. Variety can come in any area of your life—from the food you eat to the kinds of vacations you choose, from the way you do your job to the route you take to and from work.

Look for what you have left, not what you have lost. Negative thinking can cause stress, so if you consciously look for the positives in every phase of your life, you are going to have less stress. Certainly, negative events in your life cannot be overlooked because you have to deal with them, and you can learn from them; however, there is always some positive in any situation if you will look for it. When you focus on the positive in a bad situation, you are identifying *what you have left*. It does no good to focus on what was lost. For example, if your house burned down, would you bemoan what was lost or be thankful for the surviving people and possessions? What survived is now what you possess, control, and can use to build your future. Seeing the bright side is seeing the right side as far as stress is concerned.

Consider not even using the word "stress." Stress has come to mean being caught in a very strong, negative situation over which you have no control. So if you use *stress* to describe your

222

mental and physical state, you are telling your mind that you are not in control of a situation that is highly negative. Simply thinking about being in a stressful situation can trigger the run or fight mechanism, but thinking about being in an unfortunate situation or being temporarily inconvenienced should not trigger this reaction. You might even want to find a substitute for the term *stressed* that would have less of a frenzied, out-of-control connotation to you. Terms such as "concerned" or "perplexed" can connote a mental condition that is more internally-controlled and problem-solving oriented.

How you talk to yourself can make a big difference.

QUESTIONS

1. Based on your experience, do you think there are characteristics of stress other than "undesirable situation" and "out of your control"? If so, what are they? Describe them using an original example.

2. Can you describe in your own words how stress can be positive and how it can be negative? Use clear examples.

3. Would it be good or bad never to have stress in your life? Explain your answer and use examples.

4. Can you name anything that wouldn't be a possible source of stress? Remember that stress is the result of your interpretation of a situation.

5. What would you say to Frank, who is complaining to you about how much stress he is having because his boss is driving him crazy? You know Frank well and can speak openly with him.

6. Do you agree with the following statement: "How you interpret an event depends very much on your beliefs and values"? This statement refers to the equation: an event + your interpretation = your emotions. Use examples to illustrate your answer.

7. It is stated in the chapter that having negatively-thinking people near you (such as friends, fellow workers, or family) can add to your stress. Can you explain how this might happen? Be sure to give examples.

8. If someone wanted to use substitute words for stress, what word(s) would you suggest? What would be the advantage of not using the word *stress*?

9. Do you think it would be possible for someone to live his or her total life without some kind of stress? Explain your answer.

ACTIVITIES

1. Think of the times in which you would say that you are under stress. How do you know that you are feeling stressed? What are the physical or mental things that happen to you? For example, some people will have neck aches when they feel stressed. Have others in the group share their symptoms of stress. Do these symptoms seem consistent with the physiological responses to stress described in the chapter?

2. Think of a recent time in which you felt under stress. Now describe how the two major characteristics (undesirable and out of your control) are illustrated by this situation in which you were stressed. Were there other characteristics that you detected that should be added to these two?

3. Describe in your own words the difference between ancient and modern stress when you compare the hunting and gathering times to today. Now describe in what ways they are similar. Share your descriptions with others in your group. Have them give you feedback to check whether you have interpreted the differences and similarities correctly.

4. Is the formula "an event + your interpretation = your emotions" consistent with this chapter on stress? Use examples to illustrate your answer.

5. Of all the ways to prevent and reduce stress listed in this chapter, which three do you think are the most important to people of your age? Why? Share your answers and reasons in your group. Which were the most often chosen?

6. Of all the ways to prevent and reduce stress listed in this chapter, which are the most difficult for you to practice? Why? Again, share with your group and see whether there are any that have been chosen more than once.

7. List the ways to prevent and reduce stress listed in this chapter that you do not understand fully. Share these in the group and help one another understand the meaning of each of the ways to prevent or reduce stress. Also be sure that you understand the application of each way.

8. Describe how rumors, even when they are not true, can add to your stress. Use an example to illustrate your description.

9. Give an original example of how a person could treat a problem as an opportunity and be successful. Share the example and ask for feedback from the group to make it clearer.

10. Explain how cheating when taking an examination, in a business transaction, or when playing a sport can add to your stress. Use a specific and original example.

11. "Look for what you have left, not what you have lost," is an idea from this chapter. Explain in your own words how this idea works. Create a fictitious person and a fictitious set of events to illustrate the idea.

12. Can you or anyone in your group think of additional ways to prevent or reduce stress that have not been mentioned in the chapter? Be sure to share these and add them to the list.

CHAPTER 24

Sticks and Stones May Break My Bones, But Words Can Break My Heart

There is an old saying, "Sticks and stones may break my bones, but words will never hurt me." This saying was probably first spoken by a mother to her child who came home crying because some other child had called him a bad name. The mother wanted to show her child that the bad name wasn't important because it couldn't hurt the child in the way physical harm could. The mother meant well, but the statement originated a long time ago—before we knew about the power of words and the mental pictures they create. The statement simply isn't correct. We know now that words can cause deep and long-lasting psychological hurt that can be as bad as, or even worse than, physical hurt. This is true for adults but it is especially true for children.

Here is how it works. Freddy is a child who forgot his lunch at home this morning and went to school without it. His father has had to go out of his way to take the forgotten lunch to little Freddy at school. This has caused the father to change his schedule and will probably make him late for work. When the father arrives at school, Freddy is anxiously waiting for him. Angry at the inconvenience his son has caused him, the father yells at Freddy that he is stupid and inconsiderate to forget his lunch and cause his father so much trouble. Freddy unconsciously files this description of himself in his wonderful, portable computer called a brain. He automatically and immediately records, "I, Freddy, am stupid and inconsiderate." This is filed as an especially important description of himself because it comes from his father, who is a special person in the child's life. It is at this time that Freddy's father's words can break his heart. Freddy, with bowed head, slowly goes back to his classroom with his lunch in his hand and a tear in his eye.

Like all of us, Freddy also engages in self-talk. As he thinks about what just happened, he might say to himself, "Yes, I am stupid, and I am inconsiderate. In fact, I would say that I am generally a pretty worthless person. I am also forgetful. Everything happened so fast that I forgot to thank Dad for going to all the trouble of bringing my lunch to me." As Freddy thinks (talks to himself) about the situation, he takes a negative situation and makes it even more negative. He then adds even more negative images of himself. Freddy now sees himself as not only stupid and inconsiderate, but he has also added generally worthless and forgetful. If Freddy already has low self-esteem and the event were even more traumatic for him, he might continue to add many more negative images of himself.

Now add to this human mix the idea that what you think about and expect tends to come about. Freddy is thinking about himself as stupid, inconsiderate, forgetful, and generally worthless. He has mental pictures of himself being these ways, and he expects to act in these ways. His behavior during the day will tend to be consistent with the images he has of himself. As "a stupid person," he might not even try to answer the teacher's questions. As "an inconsiderate person," he might not bother to thank his friend who offers to help him with his homework. He doesn't try to remember to take the announcement of the school open house home with him because "a forgetful person" will probably forget to give it to his parents anyway. On the playground at recess, he might stay by himself because he doesn't believe other children would want to play with "a generally worthless person." This example is only about one day.

This same sequence of thoughts and actions, however, influences us throughout our lives. Someone describes us in a negative way. We record that word or phrase as a negative image of ourselves. Through self-talk, we reinforce the negative image of ourselves and even expand upon it to make our self-image more negative. We then act out those images by our behavior, which tends to be consistent with the mental image of ourselves. Our negative behavior reinforces our negative self-image and the sequence starts its negative cycle again. It seems clear that words can be as deadly to a person mentally as those sticks and stones can be physically.

It is both difficult and easy to identify the words and terms that can quickly break a person's heart and possibly lead to a lifetime of heartbreak. It is difficult because sometimes you might use a word that you think is acceptable to everyone but someone finds it hurtful and offensive. For example, you might comment regarding how strong your friend looks, but he thinks of himself as fat, and he takes your compliment as a "nice way to call me fat." You can have good intentions, but you can never be sure how others will react. On the other hand, it is relatively easy to compile a rather standard list of derogatory terms that would include such terms as stupid, ugly, lazy, dumb, clumsy, mean, dirty, sloppy, incompetent, useless, worthless, inadequate, unattractive, disgusting, slow, inept, hopeless, and other commonly used negative overgeneralizations about how people look and act.

It is also easy to make lists of derogatory terms that refer to a person's ethnicity, nationality, religion, sex, presumed intelligence, ancestors, and age. These terms also represent overgeneralizations and are often called stereotypes. These derogatory terms change over time but some seem to persist nonetheless.

What can you do about it?

- *Obviously, don't use derogatory terms.* If the term is known to be offensive to people, simply don't use it in your conversations. Can you think of any situation in which calling people derogatory names or using negative terms to describe them leads to positive consequences?

- *If you find it necessary to criticize someone,* describe the inappropriate behavior and then describe the appropriate behavior that should replace it, rather than call the person some derogatory name.

- *Think before you speak.* This is not easy to do in an emotional situation, but that is when thinking before speaking is the most important.

- *See the situation from the other person's view.* That is, have some empathy. Try to understand the other person's feelings. How would you feel if you were that person and the term you are about to use were actually said to you?

- *Don't use terms to describe others that you wouldn't want used to describe yourself.* Speak about others as you would want them to speak about you. This is an especially good place to apply the Golden Rule.

• ***Don't tolerate harmful terms being used in your presence.*** Don't condone the use of derogatory terms that can hurt others.

• ***Remember what your mother said:*** If you can't say something nice, don't say anything at all Maybe it *is* simply better not to say anything than to say something derogatory. This is not to imply that you will never use constructive criticism, but it does mean that you won't use destructive criticism.

• ***Be especially careful of what you say to children.*** They are the most vulnerable. Many adults are strong enough and wise enough to reject unjust and derogatory descriptions of themselves; however, children are much more likely to accept the negative input unquestioningly without any evaluator of it being a correct description of them. This can be especially destructive when very small children are in an environment in which they are constantly bombarded with negatives about themselves. Beginning at a very early age, they have an image of themselves as being negative people. This means that unless these negative self-images are replaced by positive images, they could live their entire lives acting out those negative images, and those negative images were placed in their minds long before they were able to comprehend them.

Cruel and inhumane people have some powerful tools if they really want to hurt someone. They can use sticks, stones, and other weapons to break skin and bones. They also have the more subtle weapons of demeaning words and terms. These words can destroy confidence, stifle initiative, rob self-esteem, create untrue negative self-images, and even "break hearts." Kind people, like us, usually resist the use of physical force; however, many of us, sometimes inadvertently and sometimes deliberately, use cruel words to those with whom we work, play, live, and love. The cruel words are just as devastating, often more so, than the physical force.

Be careful what you say—especially in anger, and especially to children.

QUESTIONS

1. What words are the most hurtful to you when others use them to describe you or your behavior? Do those words hurt you even if they are not true? In what ways can you think about those untrue words so that they won't be hurtful?

2. What words do you use sometimes that could be harmful to another person? There are probably some words you use that are harmful to others, but you just don't realize it. Should you continue to use words that you have identified as hurtful to others?

3. What does the *Golden Rule* have to do with the use of negative names and labels?

ACTIVITIES

1. Describe in your own words how (a) a negative name or label, (b) self-talk, (c) mental pictures, and (d) behavior consistent with self-image are related. Use fictitious characters in an original situation to illustrate the relationship. Share your creation with others in your group and see whether they agree with the example you illustrate. Modify your story if the relationship could be made clearer from the feedback you get from the group.

2. What words do people use about you and to you that make you feel good? Do you think others would feel better about themselves if you used these words to describe them? Of course, this assumes that the words are true descriptions of the other people and their behaviors. Be sure to share these ideas with your group. It should be very interesting to see what words make others feel good.

3. If you choose not to tolerate the use of harmful terms in your presence, how will you tell the person using the harmful terms that you do not appreciate the use of those words and will not tolerate them? Be specific. Share the ideas. Do different ideas seem appropriate for different situations, or can you find some ways of dealing with the problem in all situations?

4. See if you can create a cartoon, poem, collage, or other model to illustrate one or more of the ideas in this

chapter. Display it where others can see it or communicate it in some unique way.

5. Explain why children are more likely to be harmed by negative terms, name-calling, and labeling. Use a new set of examples to illustrate your explanation. Share your explanation with others in the group and help each other to perfect the explanations.

6. Describe how the mental harm of negative names and labeling of a person could be worse than some kinds of physical harm.

CHAPTER 25

Prevention: Not Getting INTO Trouble Is a Lot Better Than Having to Get OUT of It

It makes a great deal of sense to prevent a problem rather than having to cure it. This seems true in all phases of life. Try to think of a situation in which it would be better *not* to prevent a problem from occurring, allowing the problem to develop, and then having to solve or cure it. There may be such instances, but I haven't had that experience. In fact, I haven't even thought of one yet.

Preventing problems should be easier than solving them. It is much easier for you to eat a healthy diet than it is to be obese and have diabetes. It is easier to get an immunization than it is to get the disease and have to be cured. It is easier to fasten your seatbelt than it is to be in an automobile accident, imitate Humpty Dumpty, and be taken to an emergency room where you hopefully will be put together again.

Preventing problems should be less expensive than curing problems. It is less expensive for you to maintain your car by having recommended oil changes than it is to replace the engine. It is less expensive to consistently exercise your body than it is to have open-heart surgery. It is less expensive to spend a few minutes to find possible sources of fires in your home than it is to have a fire and suffer the human and material damages that would result.

Preventing problems should be less stressful than curing problems. For example, maintaining a home air conditioner can avoid a potentially stressful breakdown on a very hot weekend or holiday. Likewise, the stress associated with the problem of procrastination can be alleviated by doing whatever needs be done *when* it needs to be done.

Preventing problems should be less risky than letting the problems occur and then trying to cure them. Examples of this involve using tobacco, eating non-nutritious food, and getting insufficient exercise. These are all choices that people make every day, even though it is common knowledge that these habits are related to diseases of the heart and blood vessels, cancers, and emphysema, to name just a few. Even though there is medical treatment, and even if you can easily afford the costs of the best treatment available, the risks of major physical problems and even death are high. Based on the best available medical evidence you can prevent some of the highest risk diseases by breathing the cleanest air possible, eating a nutritious diet, and exercising the most fantastic machine ever invented. You can do all these by making some relatively simple changes in your lifestyle.

Perhaps the most crucial application of the concept of prevention deals with the problems that face this wonderful planet on which we live. We now have problems and risks that are global in scope. The increasing magnitude of changes, which mankind can now bring about through the uses of technology, are having global consequences. If we don't take responsibility to seek the wisdom to understand these changes and apply appropriate preventive measures, we might find that these problems are both irreversible and permanent.

Prevention is based on understanding cause and effect. Before you can effectively implement a preventive strategy, you must understand that a certain action or set of actions will have a high probability of causing a certain effect or effects in the future. Your actions lead to consequences. The consequences can be positive or negative. You can control the future consequences by your present actions. For example, you understand that the under-inflation of a car tire will cause more rapid tire wear, lower gas mileage, and increased chances of blowouts. Knowing this then leads to the choice of either preventing problems by maintaining tire pressure or disregarding prevention and suffering the consequences. The world is one huge arena of actions and consequences. Wisdom is, in large part, an awareness of these causes and effects. The more wisdom you have, the more opportunity you have to control the consequences in your life through your actions. The search for the relationships among causes and effects is the most fundamental and critical basis of a valid education.

Prevention also involves responsibility. Even if you are aware of the many causes and effects that influence your life and your world, you have to make the choice to take responsibility for using that wisdom. You can decide that the responsibility for the consequences in your life will be shaped by your deliberate choices and actions as much as possible. For example, you become convinced that it is important to understand the causes and effects that influence your life. You are convinced that this wisdom can add control and happiness to your life. You choose to take responsibility for finding as much of this wisdom as possible. You choose to change your lifestyle by being more selective in what you watch on television, in what you listen to on the radio and on recordings, and in what you read. You now choose to use these resources to develop your wisdom by defining reality rather than escaping from reality by only watching shows that entertain and do not inform you.

One of the most exciting times in this adventure we call life happens when we decide to take deliberate responsibility to increase our personal control of our journey.

The journey will be a lot less dangerous if we remember to take along a provision called prevention and if we remember to use it.

QUESTIONS

1. Can you think of any part of your life in which prevention of a problem would *not* be better than letting the problem develop and then having to solve it?

2. What are some things that you personally do to prevent problems from developing? Examples would be physical health, safety, the environment, mental health, and relationships.

3. What is the relationship between cause and effect and prevention? Can you create an original example or give a real example from your life of this relationship?

4. Can you think of someone you know who has had something bad happen to him or her that could have been easily prevented?

5. What are some fears you have? What preventive steps can you take to lessen the chance that those fears will become reality?

6. Can you think of someone you know whom you believe should be practicing some kind of prevention to avoid a problem that you see but perhaps he or she does not see?

ACTIVITIES

1. By yourself or in a small group, make a list of some of the major problems in your neighborhood, city, state, nation, or in the world. Choose at least three different problems and determine what caused them. Then see if you can figure out how the problems could have been prevented.

2. Discuss the statement, "Deliberate human actions always have some consequences to the person performing the action and frequently have consequences to people who never even knew the action occurred." Do you think this is true? Can you give examples? Are there exceptions to the statement? How does the statement relate to prevention?

3. Choose a problem that interests you or your group if you are in one. Can you determine whether it would have been easier, less expensive, less stressful, or less risky to prevent it?

4. What behavior could you begin to do now that would probably prevent or lessen a problem that you don't want to have happen?

CHAPTER 26

The Pursuit of Money: Some Benefits and Limitations

Many people think that money is the main route to happy and successful lives. Some of these people spend their lives working in jobs they dislike because they chose their work on the basis of making money rather than on job satisfaction. A few people have even married for money rather than for qualities such as compatibility, compassion, and companionship. Other people steal, cheat, and commit all sorts of crimes to get money. Wars have been fought, in large part, for economic reasons. Money, or wealth if you prefer, is the major motivating force in many people's lives. Before you allow the pursuit of money to be the dominant purpose in your life, perhaps you should think about the limitations of money as well as the benefits of money. The following ideas are meant to put money in a somewhat more realistic perspective.

Money is a means, and not an end, in itself. Money itself has no value. You can accumulate all the money in the world, but it is useless unless you use it in some way. Money is simply a medium of exchange that can be used to purchase goods and services. Our society has become too complicated to trade goods and services, so we use money to make it easy to make economic transactions. The more money you have, the more goods and services you can buy. If there were no goods or services to buy, your money would be worthless.

Money cannot guarantee you happiness. Money can buy you goods and services only. To the extent that the goods and services make you happy, money can contribute to your happiness. Money can secure you a comfortable home, dependable transportation, recreation, health care, and all of the other things that we usually think of as basic standards for a reasonably good life in the United States today; however, it is the way you think about these things that will make you happy—not the things themselves. For example, you may not be happy with your comfortable home because you compare it to the nicer home of your friend. You may be unhappy with your present car because it is not as luxurious as your previous car. You may be able to afford a two-week vacation to Paris but not enjoy it when it rains for one of the weeks that you are there. Money only gives you additional opportunities for happiness. Your ultimate degree of happiness, or lack of it, will depend much more on how you interpret those opportunities rather than on the opportunities you choose. What you think and how you think about your life do not have to depend on wealth.

Money allows you more choices in your life. Wealthy people have more choices in their lives than poorer people do. For example, a poorer person who wants to dine out might be restricted to once or twice a week at a fast-food chain restaurant. Wealthy people might be able to eat out any time they feel like it and at any of the restaurants in town. Wealthy people also have more choices in the levels of education they might wish to pursue. They have better chances of finishing higher levels of education, and this greater education opens up more choices for them in choosing their vocations. In contrast, the poorer person with a lesser education has fewer job choices. In terms of any goods or services, the wealthy person will always have more choices than the poorer person. The person with money can make the same choices as the person without money, but the same range of choices is simply not available to the poorer person. Having more choices allows you more opportunity for variety in life, but it doesn't guarantee that your choices will be for variety or that those choices will lead to more happiness.

Wealth allows you to purchase luxuries that can be harmful to you. Some people choose to use their money to purchase items such as tobacco, alcohol, and other drugs that are harmful to their personal health. These substances also can lead to problems that involve others in their family and society. For example, some people will purchase tobacco and liquor rather than purchase wholesome food for themselves or their families. Another example is the immoral act of driving after using alcohol or other drugs and putting the lives of innocent people in jeopardy. Money not only does not ensure happiness but its use, as described above, can almost ensure long-term unhealthiness and unhappiness. Be careful that your use of money to gain short-term pleasure does not result in long-term disaster to yourself or others.

Money can purchase you time to pursue the things you really love to do. Likewise, if you have enough money, you might hire someone to do the things you dislike doing. For example, if you dislike house cleaning but love to make pottery, you might hire someone to do the house cleaning to give you time to take a pottery class. Wealthy people can use their money to substitute the pleasurable for what they find unpleasant.

Many of the happiest people are those who have chosen their work for the pleasure they experience rather than the monetary reward. They operate on the theory that you should choose work that you love. If you do that, you will automatically have pleasure and happiness in your life because much of your waking life is spent doing the work you love. This theory goes on to suggest that if you love your work, you will do it well and that work done well will usually be well-rewarded. This is certainly the best of both worlds, and it is an idea that you should take seriously. If you are in school and are pondering choices of future vocations, it might be well advised to use enjoyment and interest as some of your main criteria for judging among the alternatives; however, the wise decision-maker will also take monetary reward into consideration. It would be totally unwise to choose a livelihood selling a product or service that no one will purchase. The same is true if you are now in a job that you don't find enjoyable or interesting. It's never too late to find a job that you love to do and that you will do well. For too long, work has been thought of as only a way to make a living instead of a way to enjoy life and make a living at the same time.

You don't need money to indulge in many, and perhaps most, of life's pleasures. When people are asked about the things that make them the happiest, they are usually quite surprised that their pleasures are not as expensive as they would have guessed. Some of the happiest times in their lives are built around the everyday human relationships they have with their family, friends, and other companions. Others cite the simple enjoyments of sunsets, interesting conversation, music, aromas, pets, art, literature, a warm drink on a cold day, a refreshing shower, the crunch of new snow underfoot, watching a child play, and humor as examples of the many delightful aspects of our lives that are readily available to nearly all of us every day. The search for happiness does not have to rely on money for its successful completion.

A poor person's disaster is a wealthy person's inconvenience. Having an adequate amount of money can lead to a less stressful life. For example, if you are a poorer person and your automobile needs a new transmission during a holiday when you already have some added expenses, it can potentially be a very stressful situation for you. If you were a person with more money, however, it would be an undesirable situation but would represent an inconvenience to you rather than a major financial hardship. Having wealth can soften the unexpected financial blows that all of us encounter.

Money itself can't change you inside. If a person thought of herself as being stupid and ugly, she wouldn't start thinking of herself as being smart and beautiful if she won a lot of money in the lottery. A person with low self-esteem will not gain high self-esteem by simply inheriting money. Again, money can only purchase goods and services. You cannot purchase self-esteem; however, money might allow you to make choices, such as changing to a job you love, which can lead to the accomplishments and successes that increase your self-esteem and happiness.

Money can buy outside physical changes by using procedures like facelifts, hairstyles, tummy tucks, and liposuction. These don't necessarily involve any inner changes, however. Money can't buy the attitudinal and other mental changes that are important to your happiness. Only you can make the important changes—the inner changes.

Money can buy you more now, but you will probably just want more later. We humans are very interesting. Our happiness seems to be measured in comparison to something. For example, let us pretend that you never had a bicycle before. You always had to walk or hitch a ride or use public transportation. Now you obtain the money to buy a nice used and dependable three-speed bicycle. You are quite happy because you now have more freedom of movement. You are happy for several weeks until you see that other people have bicycles with ten gears that make it much easier to go up hills. Now you are not so happy with your bicycle because you are comparing your bicycle to one with more gears rather to the times when you had to walk. You now feel that you will be much happier when you get a bicycle with more gears. You watch the papers and are able to find and purchase a nearly new ten-speed bicycle that makes you somewhat happier because it is a little easier to pedal up hills. After some time, you notice several scratches on your bicycle and note that the tires are beginning to wear a little. You have the money to purchase a new bike, and you do so. This bicycle, although new, does not bring you the joy that you thought it would. Notice that each time that you purchased something more expensive, it became a standard of comparison for judging your happiness. Once you became accustomed to the used three-speed bike, happiness was getting a bike that had more gears. Finally, the used bike had to be replaced with a new bike for you to be happy. This constant escalation of comparisons of things money can buy suggests that happiness is always just one purchase away, no matter how many things we purchase. The way to stop this escalation, of course, is to enjoy what you have now compared to what you didn't have before, rather than to compare what you have now with what you don't have.

The more money you have, the more difficult it might be to gain happiness by purchasing things. As we purchase more and more expensive things, the margin for happiness narrows because the difference in the items narrows. Using the example above, there was a large difference between having a bicycle and not having a bicycle. This gained you the most happiness. There was less difference between the three-speed and the ten-speed bikes, and you gained less happiness than you did when you purchased your first bike. There was even less difference between your used ten-speed bike and your new ten-speed bike. This was your smallest gain in happiness, and it might have even been a bit disappointing. You would probably find the same thing to be true if you were buying an iPod or an iPhone, automobiles, hair dryers, carpets, or anything else that money can buy. The more expensive they are, the less the real difference in them. Perhaps that is why, as your wealth increases, it becomes more difficult to be happy if your happiness is based on what money can buy. Maybe there is such a thing as being too rich.

Maybe you already have enough. There is a saying that comes from the country of Tanzania. Translated from Swahili, it says something like, "Isn't there a time in your life when you have enough and you can then turn your attention from getting more for yourself to helping others?" Perhaps this is especially appropriate for us in this country. When do you have enough? Does it make sense to keep acquiring more and more wealth far beyond what you need? If you think about it, maybe you already have enough to make you happy. Maybe you already have enough "stuff" and getting more will only give marginal benefits that aren't worth what else you could be doing with your life.

What could you be doing with your life?

QUESTIONS

1. How do you respond to the old saying, "The love of money is the root of all evil"? Agree? Disagree? What else could be at the root of human evil?

2. Depending on how it is used, could money be the root of good actions and activity by humans?

3. Where does money fit in your life? What would rank more important than money to you?

4. What is the most important thing that money can buy you at this point in your life?

5. What are some of the worst things you have seen other people purchase with their money?

6. What are some of the best uses of money you have seen?

7. What were some of your foolish or "poor" uses of money?

8. What are some of your wisest uses of money, uses of which you are most proud?

9. If you were given $1 million right now, what would you do with it? How would you determine whether you were using this money wisely?

10. Do you think people can be happy without much money? How could this be?

11. Where have you gotten your ideas about money and its value? Do you think these are the best sources of information? Where might you gain more information to help you plan your financial future?

12. If you are in a vocation now, on what criteria did you choose it? To what degree did you choose it for gaining money? How do you feel about your choice now? Would you change your decision if you had the chance? Is it too late if you feel uncomfortable with your earlier decisions?

13. If you have not chosen your vocation yet, what role should money play in that choice? Some people who have already made this decision have found they did not emphasize making money as much as they should have and just chose something they liked to do. Others chose the highest paying job and hoped they could tolerate it. Maybe there is a happy medium in which you can find an enjoyable vocation that also has a good salary! What percentages of money potential and enjoyment potential should you use in your choice?

ACTIVITIES

1. Make a personal list of all the things you could purchase that could be harmful to you in the long run, even though they could be pleasurable in the short run. Share your list with others in the group. Make a group list by adding together your individual lists.

2. Make a personal list of the most important goods or services that you could purchase with your money. Again, share these in the group and make a master list of important uses of wealth by adding all of your lists together. Analyze your master list and determine whether the items would be more likely to lead to short-term happiness, long-term happiness, or both.

3. Choose a limited time, such as ten or fifteen minutes, and during that time write down all of the things you love to do that do not require money or that require very little. It is important that you share your list with others in the group and that they share with you because you might discover some inexpensive pleasures that you hadn't thought of before. If you discover some new pleasurable activities that are inexpensive or cost no money, be sure to try some of them.

4. Have your group discuss the idea that for some people, "Happiness is just one purchase away." Can you think of examples of this that you have seen in your life? What are the implications of this as a way of life?

5. Have each person in the group explain the idea that purchasing expensive versions in the same category of something can lead to less satisfaction with each increasingly costly purchase. Each explanation should be illustrated by an original example. When the examples have been exchanged, discuss what alternatives might be more desirable uses of one's wealth.

6. Discuss the idea from Tanzania that "there should be a time in your life when you have enough and you can then turn your attention from getting more for yourself to helping others." Do you agree with it? Is it practical in today's economy? How much is enough?

CHAPTER 27

Don't Confuse Form and Substance

Many years ago a document needed to be completed. It was not especially important information, but someone in the bureaucracy wanted it. To save time, I neatly printed the information in the blanks. I print very neatly, and it was quite easy to read. The completed document was sent. In a few days, the document came back with a terse message that the blanks must be completed in typing. I immediately returned the original neatly-printed document, pointing out that I had supplied the information requested and that it was a waste of my time to re-copy that information with a typewriter.

This is an excellent example of why the differences between substance and form need to be understood. In the example above, the substance of the communication was the information that was supplied in the blanks. In this case, it was communicated by neatly printing the information rather than typing the information. The bureaucrat's concern was more about how the relatively unimportant document was written (form) rather than what was written (substance) in the document. I later discovered that someone was asked to copy my printing onto a new document using a typewriter. This was a waste of human and institutional resources based, at least in part, on a lack of understanding of the differences between substance and form. This kind of waste occurs in various forms many times every day. I hope this chapter will make these differences clearer so that we can all save some of our precious time and limited resources.

In any situation, there is probably substance and form. They are not always easy to identify. According to a dictionary, the substance of something is "the essential nature of it," "the essence of it," or "the fundamental part or quality." Another way to define substance is by "the usefulness of it," "the practical importance of something," "its meaning," or "its basic purpose." For practice, use the example above and see how it applies to the substance definitions quoted in this paragraph. Do you see how the information I supplied in the blanks fits each one of the definitions of substance?

The form of something is easier for most of us to distinguish. It is defined as "the shape of something," "the structure of something," or "the external appearance." These definitions mostly refer to things and objects. Form is also often identified as the "means by which something is done" or the "way something is done." These definitions are usually most appropriate for applying to our activities and behavior. In the example above, the form (either hand-printed or typed) is the way in which the information (substance) was written. The following are several examples and explanations of substance and form.

The substance (basic purpose) of a car is to transport human beings from one place to another. The forms are all the different models, colors, sizes, and options that are offered by automobile manufacturers. If you believe the purpose of the car (substance) is transportation, you will look for one that will transport you safely, economically, and with as few problems as possible. If you judge the car by form, you are more likely to base your purchase on body shape, color, and other features of appearance. People who have bought that "cute little red car" because of its form often have been sorry when it has cost them time and money in unanticipated repairs or even led to injury.

The substance of school is the knowledge that students acquire to enable them to gain control over their lives. Form refers to the many ways in which teachers lead students to interact with that knowledge and convey that knowledge to the students. When schools emphasize the substance (the knowledge), they are most concerned with the value of what is being taught. When schools concentrate on form, they are most concerned with how the knowledge is taught. If the concern is mostly form rather than substance, it could result in the schools teaching relatively valueless subject matter but teaching it very well. This example shows why it is important to consider the substance as more important than the form.

Many people choose a companion and even get married largely because of physical appearance (form). They often find later that the substance of the person is not as desirable as their appearance. Desirable substantive qualities such as being a caring person, having a sense of humor, being an interesting person, having empathy, being honest, and being dependable are often lacking even though the person is physically very attractive. External appearance is no guarantee of internal substance.

An example from my personal life involves furniture. In looking for a sofa to purchase several years ago, I found one that looked beautiful. It was the right color and it fit perfectly with the decor of our home. The form of it was great. How about the substance? A sofa is for comfortable seating. When I sat in it, it wasn't really very comfortable and the seat cushions seemed to slip out from under me if I moved a little. The substance wasn't great at all; however, it had just the right look for our living room, and it was on sale! *I ignored the substance and bought the form.* The result was that this sofa looked great but nobody wanted to sit on it, and when anyone did sit on it, the cushions kept sliding forward and off.

Think of situations in your life in which you have made decisions or where you will be making decisions in the future. See if you can separate the substance from the form in these situations. Do you see a pattern in your decision-making?

Do you tend to make decisions more on the basis of substance or form?

The following are some ideas about substance and form that you might find to be important as you apply these concepts to your life.

Form is usually easier to detect than substance, so don't get discouraged if it seems difficult at first. The form is almost always identified as the package in which the substance is delivered or as the way in which the substance is delivered. Water comes disguised in forms of liquids, solids, and vapors. A message can be delivered in many different forms, such as letter, telephone call, email, fax, television, texting, social media, and face-to-face conversation.

Form is usually easier to change than substance. This may be the reason that most schools have had more success changing how they teach, but have had less success in changing what is taught. It is easier to change the shape of an automobile than it is to change more substantive aspects such as its safety, dependability, and mileage.

Many arguments could be avoided or lessened by keeping substance and form differences in mind. For example, one person could be arguing substance and another arguing form, and they will never be able to come to an agreement. Joe could be arguing that the new Blastem sound system is not good because it has terrible sound (substance), and he wouldn't buy one. His friend, Sam, says he would buy the Blastem system because it is small enough for him to carry and it comes in wonderful colors (form). Joe is using a substance criterion for making his judgment, and Sam is using two form criteria for making his judgment. They are arguing from completely different positions, and they are both logically correct. They will not be able to come to a mutual agreement, however, when they are using such different criteria to judge the worth of the sound system. *When they understand this, they can agree to disagree and stop their argument.* If they don't recognize the difference between their positions, they could argue forever.

Although both substance and form can often be satisfied, it is substance that must always be emphasized. Substance is the priority. Without substance, the form is relatively unimportant. Who wants to have their children taught unimportant school subjects with wonderful methods? Who wants to have a beautiful car that won't run? Who wants to have a physically attractive spouse whose company they can't enjoy? Who wants to live a life chasing forms that have no substance?

Perhaps we all need to do a little evaluating of our lives. How much of what we do is substance? How much is form? Are our goals mostly based on form or substance? It is not always easy to distinguish form from substance. It is not always easy to keep substance as a priority when form is usually more obvious. It is not always easy making the more difficult changes that involve substance when it is usually easier to change the form. It is not always easy to analyze and plan our lives.

But in the long run, it's worth it. And it's a lot more effective as well.

QUESTIONS

1. Have you ever been in a situation in which form and substance were misunderstood, and this misunderstanding evolved into a problem? How could that problem have been avoided if you had understood the differences between form and substance at that time?

2. What reasons can you think of for being able to distinguish between form and substance? Can you give at least one example of each of your answers?

3. Do you believe that substance is more important than form? If not, why not? Can you think of any situation in which form is more important than substance?

ACTIVITIES

1. Indicate in the space whether the sentence describes form (mark an "F") or substance (mark an "S").

    _____The shoe is very comfortable.

    _____The book has 250 pages and a hard cover.

    _____The auto mechanic has good advertisements on television.

    _____The sandwich tastes good and is nutritious.

    _____The teacher always teaches at least one thing students can use to improve their lives.

    _____This new phone is made to look like a shoe.

    _____The belt is made of beautiful black leather.

2. In the following sentences, indicate which part refers to the form (underline the form section with one line) and/or which part refers to substance (underline the substance section with two lines). Be able to explain your answers to others in the group. There is no one correct answer on some of the descriptions because your answer will depend on what you interpret as being most important (substance) in that particular situation.

    My big green car would not start.

    My beautiful girlfriend never pays much attention to me when other guys are around.

    My clothes are comfortable and I like the way they look.

My heavy winter coat doesn't keep me very warm and my friends tell me that it is also very ugly.

3. Write a short description of an event that involves people about your age having an argument in which one argues from the side of form and the other argues from the side of substance. Some suggested events might be choosing clothes, evaluating a book that both have read, helping someone who is buying a car, or choosing a restaurant. When you have finished your description, read it to another person or to the group and see if they can tell which part of your story is about form and which is about substance. Each of you should take turns until all of the papers have been read. Help the writer of each story rewrite it, if needed, to make the form and substance descriptions very clear.

4. Choose someone in the group to start by naming an object (car, tool, house, train, glass, fork, dog, or rock). Then go around the group and have each person name one substance and one form characteristic for that object. Take some time to think about it and write down answers before you start taking turns. If you disagree about someone's characteristics, be sure to indicate it so that you can analyze the disagreement and determine a clear characteristic. Remember that you are trying to have clear examples of substance and form.

5. Can you create a visual way to illustrate form and substance and the differences between them? Show your creation to someone else and see whether they understand what you

have done without explanation. If they don't understand, have them describe how they would have done it differently.

CHAPTER 28

Self-Discipline: The Strength to Control Yourself

Self-discipline can be defined as "doing something you believe to be right even when it is inconvenient and even if nobody is looking." Look at the first part of this definition about regulating oneself: "doing something you believe to be right." If you are a self-disciplined person, you behave as you do because you are convinced that those actions are valuable and worthwhile. For example, you would not drink and drive because you know that puts your life and the lives of others at risk. You don't do something simply because others do it or because someone has told you to do it. As a self-disciplined person, you wouldn't drink and drive even if your friends urged you to and even if they pointed out that everybody else does it. *Your behavior has to make sense to you before you will do it.* It has to have value to you and you have to be convinced that it won't be harmful in some way to others or yourself. Self-disciplined people are strong, moral people who think about their behavior as well as the consequences of their behaviors.

The second part of the definition states, "even when it is inconvenient." Self-disciplined people do what they think is right even if it isn't the easiest or most fun thing they could be doing at the moment. For example, suppose you decided that it would be good for your health and your looks if you exercised more. You decide that part of this exercise will involve your swimming 40 laps every other day. As a self-disciplined person, you would swim your 40 laps every other day even though it would be easier not to do it. You discipline yourself to remain on this schedule even though you could be taking a nap, watching television, reading a book, or strolling in a park instead of swimming those laps; however, you are willing to discipline yourself now because you believe that you will feel and look better in the future. You are willing to postpone immediate gratifications now for greater gratification in the future. Swimming laps might not be your favorite thing to do, but you are willing to do it because you want to have more energy, and you want to like what you see when you look in the mirror.

Note that this does not mean that self-disciplined people have no fun. Delaying gratification is a deliberate choice to make an investment in time, energy, money, or some other resource now in order to achieve a greater gratification or more fun at some later time. A good example is saving some of your money rather than spending it all as soon as you get it. You invest it and, as a result, have more money to spend at a later time. Hopefully, you will spend the larger sum of money in ways that will give you greater satisfaction and make you happier than if you had simply spent the original money on the day you got it.

It should also be noted that delaying gratification need not be a total delay. You can have some fun swimming laps, and you can spend some money for fun now. *Self-discipline does not mean that you will be totally unhappy now so that you can be totally happy later.* The trick is to look for and find as much happiness as possible in everything you do. Think of delaying gratification as a matter of degree, not as a total absence of fulfillment. Something can be inconvenient, but you can still find some pleasure or enjoyment from it. This is simply another example of looking for the positive in a situation instead of looking for the negative in a situation. If you can become really expert at finding the good in every situation, you would never have to have delayed gratification because you could always find some gratification in everything. All that takes is a change in thinking.

The third part of the definition states, "even if nobody is looking." This means that self-disciplined people do what they believe to be right even if there is no authority to watch them and make sure they do it. They do what they think to be correct even if there is no one there to reward them. For example, the self-disciplined person eats nutritious food to be healthy, not because he will get dessert if he cleans his plate of the vegetables and fruit first. The self-disciplined person does what she thinks is correct even when there is no one there to punish her if she doesn't do it. For example, the self-disciplined driver obeys the traffic laws because obeying the laws increases the safety for herself and others, not because she is afraid of being caught by the police.

How do you act if you are not self-disciplined? *If you are not disciplining or controlling yourself, you are being controlled by others or you are unable to control yourself.* When you are being controlled by others, you do things because others reward or punish you in some way. For example, you might know it is wrong to spread gossip because it can hurt people, but you do it anyway because your best friend enjoys talking about people behind their backs. To keep the friendship, you also spread rumors even though you know it is wrong. You choose the reward of friendship from one "friend" to control this part of your behavior.

We sometimes allow others to control our lives in this way because we do not have the confidence in ourselves to risk their possible anger or disappointment. We find it is more difficult to act independently of what others might think of us than it is to believe in ourselves and our judgment and do what

269

we think is right. Are there situations in your life in which you do something for the reward or out of fear of punishment, even though you don't feel good about doing it?

Sometimes we are not self-disciplined because we are unable to restrain or control ourselves. We do things we know are not in our best interests. For example, we abuse our bodies with tobacco, alcohol, fats, sugars, salt, and huge quantities of food even though we are aware of the evidence that they are harmful to us. Rather than restrict or discontinue these physical abuses, we continue them, hoping that we will not be the ones who will eventually pay the negative consequences of this lack of self-restraint. Why can't we control our own behavior? Why can't we restrain ourselves from what we know is self-destructive behavior?

We often don't have self-control because of the ways we think and the beliefs we have. For example, we will find it very difficult to change destructive habits when we believe "that's how I have always done it." We cannot have the self-discipline to make difficult changes in our lives when we believe that "you can't teach an old dog new tricks" or "that's just the way I am." Although we all have the power to change our lives, we often have beliefs such as these that program us to accept ourselves as unable to be in charge of our lives. Do you have any such beliefs?

If we aren't self-disciplined, we often choose to take what appears to us at the time as the easy way out. We know what we are supposed to do but rather than do that, we do something that seems to be easier. Perhaps the best examples of not being self-disciplined are times in which we procrastinate. We have all put off writing that paper for school, calling someone we didn't want to call, confronting someone of whom we were fearful, or changing a habit we knew was working against our best interests. We know we need to do something, but we put it off to a later time. We try to ignore the fact that the task will still be there for us to do. We try to ignore the fact that we feel uneasy, if not guilty, for not doing it. We know that we will have to do it eventually, but we still put it off. We know we will feel better when we finally do the task, but we continue to postpone it. During the time we postpone the task, we often worry about it and are unable to enjoy what we are doing instead of doing the task. What seems to be the easy way out becomes the miserable and stressful way out. If we were self-disciplined, we would do what we believe needs to be done *when* it needs to be done. Then we would have the wonderful feeling of accomplishing something important, and we would be able to enjoy ourselves without the stress of knowing that we aren't doing something we should be doing. Self-discipline can take a lot of stress out of our lives. Self-discipline usually is the easy way out in the long run.

People who are not self-disciplined often cheat themselves. For example, self-disciplined people who want to eat nutritious diets eat nutritious foods all the time (with the exception of a deliberate splurge once in a while) whether someone is watching them or not. On the other hand, non-self-disciplined people eat nutritious foods when others are looking but eat large quantities of non-nutritious foods when they are alone and no one can see them. They are actually cheating themselves out of a nutritious diet and some degree of health. The same thing is true of the people who do not follow through with such personal programs as exercise, oral hygiene, weight maintenance, and lifelong education. The lack of self-discipline in areas such as these often leads to less-than-desirable physical and mental health. This is often visible as illness, unattractiveness, and low self-esteem. Many of these problems could be avoided if we would use our self-discipline to do what we know is right—even when it is inconvenient and even if no one is watching over us.

The lack of self-discipline can be harmful to other people. For example, the automobile mechanic, who does not check all of the items on the 20-item safety inspection of your car because he is too tired and his supervisor is not watching, could overlook something that causes you to have an accident. The cook in the restaurant might spread disease to many people if he doesn't wash his hands after going to the bathroom, even though there is a sign in the restroom to remind him that cleaning his hands is necessary. He doesn't wash his hands because it is too much trouble and, besides, who will know? Another example is the way in which people can be harmed when we do not have the self-discipline to carry out the promises we make to them.

The lack of self-discipline is harmful to our environment. Self-discipline on all of our parts could lessen the air and water pollution, decrease waste, and conserve our limited resources. This would require that each of us does what we know is right, even if it is inconvenient and especially when no one is watching.

Think of all the people whom you trust every day to do what they are supposed to do even if it is an inconvenience to them and even when they aren't being supervised. Be thankful that so many people are self-disciplined.

Now think of all the people, especially yourself, who trust you to do what you know is right even though it might inconvenience you and even when no one is watching.

Do they, and especially you, have reason to be thankful for your self-discipline?

QUESTIONS

1. What is your definition of self-discipline in your own words? How does it differ from the definition in this book?

2. What are some reasons that people should practice self-control? Would there be situations in which a person should neither practice nor be aware of self-control?

3. What do you suppose the world would be like if there was no self-discipline? Give some examples.

4. How do laws and rules relate to self-discipline?

5. Can you think of any ways that procrastination might be related to self-discipline?

6. Do you tend to act differently when someone else is looking as compared to being alone? Under what circumstances (for example, eating, doing chores around the house, or working)? Is it important who is watching?

7. Give an original example of ways in which someone (you?) might cheat himself or herself by not being self-disciplined.

ACTIVITIES

1. Sometimes our friends encourage us to do things that we know we should not do. What are some of those situations that you have heard about or observed? Make a list of these from all of the members of your group. Which do you think would be the most difficult to handle? Which ones would be relatively easy to handle? What factors are most important in determining the ease with which you deal with a situation? An example would be fear that your friends will not like you if you don't behave as the group wants you to behave.

2. Sometimes our friends discourage us from doing things we know we should do. What are some of those situations you have heard about or observed? Make a list of these situations from all of the members of the group. Which do you think would be the most difficult to handle? Which ones would be relatively easy to handle? What factors are most important in determining the ease with which you deal with the situations?

3. Write a short description of someone about your age who is put into a situation in which self-discipline is needed. Then introduce your character to someone who tries to discourage the use of his or her self-discipline. Now describe what your character does. Are the consequences for your character good or bad? Be creative. Did your character pass the self-discipline test?

4. List ways in which people behave when they are not self-disciplined. For example, a person who was not self-disciplined might act without thinking of the consequences of his or her actions on other people. Make a group list of these undisciplined behaviors. Which ones are potentially the most harmful?

5. Make a list of the times you can remember in which you somehow cheated yourself by not practicing self-discipline.

6. Make a list of times in which you somehow caused harm to or hurt someone else because you did not practice self-discipline.

7. Make a list of the ways in which people cause harm to the environment because they do not practice self-discipline. Which of those harmful practices do you think does the most harm to animals in the environment? Which does the most harm to our water? What other specific parts of the environment are harmed by these undisciplined acts?

8. Do you agree with the following statement, "Self-discipline is more important when you live in a society of people than if you live alone"? What are your reasons?

9. On a scale of one to ten (with ten being the highest), how would you rate yourself on being trusted to be self-

disciplined? In what situations are you most likely to be self-disciplined? When is it most difficult for you to be self-disciplined? What have been the results of your lack of self-discipline in these situations?

10. Can you illustrate one or more important ideas about self-discipline in a cartoon, drawing, painting, or any other visual medium?

11. What do you believe would be the most harmful kind of lack of self-discipline possible? Have everyone share his or her answer. Is one a clear winner?

12. What do you believe are the five most important things about which a person your age should be self-disciplined? Share your ideas in the group and make a master list. Compare your list to the master list of the group. Would you change your list in any way now? Why?

CHAPTER 29

The Courage to be Different

Everybody wants to fit in. Everybody wants to be liked. We all want to have friends. Our need to be accepted leads many of us to conform to the way we believe others want us to act. We know people are usually most comfortable with us when we are like them. They like people who look like them, think like them, and act like them. Isn't this true of the groups with which you are familiar? Don't the people in them tend to look alike with similar clothes, hair, and other grooming styles? Don't they tend to share the same beliefs? Don't they tend to act similarly in social situations and have many common habits? If you or I want to be part of these groups, we have to conform to at least some of the group's characteristics. If we choose to be different from what the group considers to be normal, we are also probably choosing to be rejected by the group or by some of its members.

Most of the time we do whatever is required to be accepted. We don't think much about it. We just go along with what everybody else is doing. Before long, we all look, think, and act pretty much the same. Where do you fit? Look at your own life. To what degree have you unquestioningly conformed to the clothes, grooming, looks, beliefs, and behaviors of the groups to which you belong? Did you choose these lifestyles deliberately, or did they just sort of happen? Do you make thoughtful choices, or do you just do what most people do? In what ways are you like everybody else, and in what ways are you different? Should you be different? Can you afford to be different? *Do you have the courage to be different?*

The following are ideas about conformity and being different.

It is normal to want to fit in, be liked, and be accepted. The need to belong is basic in little children, adolescents, and adults. Being accepted is a fundamental human drive.

It is normal to conform in some ways to be like the people around you so that you can be accepted by those people. This is probably strongest during the adolescent years when the need for acceptance, especially from peers, is most pronounced. Teenager groups have many rituals of grooming, dress, language, and manners, which require a high degree of conformity if one is to gain acceptance into a specific group.

Anyone can be an unthinking follower. It doesn't take any talent just to go along with the crowd. Conforming often seems the right thing to do in the short run; however, in the long run, it can be costly to the individual and society. Being an unthinking follower costs us our human potential. You have to build on your unique individual interests and strengths if you are to use your potential to the fullest. Leaders in making positive change are *not* unthinking followers.

It takes courage to be different. It takes courage for the youngster to continue to practice his musical instrument when all of his friends are playing baseball. It takes courage for

278

the teenage girl to participate in family events when all of her friends are rejecting their parents. It takes courage for the young man to stay in school when all of his friends are dropping out, getting jobs, and making money. It takes courage to speak against prejudice when all of your friends hate anyone with a different shade of skin color. It takes courage for the scientist to share his new findings when they go against all of the current theories in his field.

People who are different see the world in different or non-normal ways. Their "differentness" in perception lets them think in unique ways. They make breakthroughs because they see in ways that "normal" people don't see. They also make interesting, if not sometimes dangerous, friends— dangerous in that being different is often punished, at least initially.

Be kind to those who are different. Encourage responsible nonconformity. These people are the ones who will make the positive changes in our world. They will give up some of their acceptance from others by being different, and they can use your friendship and understanding.

Breakthroughs are made by people who are different. Every major change in the world was brought about by someone who was different. Most of us think of inventions when we think of breakthroughs. We think of inventors such as Robert Fulton, Alexander Graham Bell, Thomas Edison, Albert Einstein, and Eli Whitney. They had to be different and think differently because what they did had never been done before. There were always people around who were telling them that they were crazy and what they were trying to do would never work.

The same thing probably happened to whomever invented the wheel. The same ridicule probably was heaped on the people who conceived the idea of democracy (most certainly by the monarchy). Many of the people we most honor now were thought of as crackpots when they first introduced the ideas that eventually made them famous. This is why we have to listen to those who are different. We at least have to give them a chance to be heard. Give them the same chance to be heard that you would like to have when *you* have an idea that can change the world.

It takes a strong and secure person to be different, and it takes a strong and secure person to allow others to be different. The more insecure and unsure a person is, the more likely the person is to conform. It is less threatening for them to be like everybody else. It is also difficult for the insecure person to tolerate different people. Insecurity breeds intolerance of different people and different ideas. Strong and secure people see diversity as a great way to meet different people and learn new ideas. Secure people promote differences knowing they will be enriched by these differences.

You are too important to let others dictate your life, even if they do it with the best of intentions. You need to take responsibility for the choices in your life. Other people, no matter how sincere they seem, do not necessarily know what is good for you. Listen to the advice they give and learn from the models they provide, but *always keep the final decision for yourself.* You are the one who will have to live with the decisions— whether you make them or not.

If you choose to be different, you might encounter trouble. Many people do not like people who are different from them. They do not like people who have different customs, religions, shades of skin color, physical features, or nationalities, but they are especially fearful of new ideas. These people are full of prejudices and, if you are different, they might cause some

280

kind of trouble for you. People who have chosen to be different have suffered throughout history. Their sufferings range from isolation and ridicule to torture and death. Those who choose to be different are more tolerated today, but they must be prepared for the discrimination that often goes with not being like everybody else.

Normal or average is not good or bad. You want to be normal in some things. For example, the normal person obeys the laws; however, a study indicates that the average American family watches nearly eight hours of television a day. This is normal behavior, but it is not very wise or good behavior.

Creativity is being different. Creativity is seeing your world through new perspectives. It is arranging your experiences into new combinations. Sometimes it is combining those experiences into arrangements that no one has ever done before. When you are creative, you might be seen as eccentric and odd because you must think differently from others if you are going to create. We don't have to like what is created, but we must tolerate, respect, and encourage the qualities of uniqueness so that creativity is possible.

You don't choose to be different just to be different. You choose to be different because you believe in something or somebody so much that you are willing to risk being rejected by your peers who believe otherwise. You don't set out to be different to draw attention deliberately to yourself. Being different is a byproduct of pursuing something you believe in even when nobody else shares your belief. Being different just to draw attention to yourself is usually a sign of immature behavior.

Being different is not an excuse for irresponsible behavior. Responsible differentness is standing up for and pursuing something you deem valuable however unpopular it is with others. Some people try to disguise their irresponsible behavior as being only different behavior, however. For example, a person who is a chronic procrastinator says that he is just different and people don't understand him. He wants us to believe that he is being unjustly criticized for simply being different in the hope that we will overlook his irresponsible procrastination. The same kind of excuse is often heard from substance abusers and others who exercise little self-discipline. Responsible differences are to be encouraged; however, the acceptance of differences as an excuse for irresponsible behavior helps no one.

We sometimes conform to a small group to be different from a large group. A good example of this occurs when people want to show how different they are from normal society in their ideas, behaviors, and looks. In order to show their differences they form small groups (hippies, punk rockers, political groups, clubs, to name a few) in which they share and conform to the sub-group's goals, appearances, and ideas. They stand as very different from the larger society. An interesting pattern often evolves whereby nonconformists organize, become popular, eventually become the majority, and then want to outlaw behaviors different from their way of life.

Be a student of the normal and average. Be a researcher of what most other people are doing. Discover what most people need and provide it. See what most people are doing and do something different. Perhaps this is a way in which you can find a niche for your business, vocation, or some of your many talents. A radical but provocative suggestion is to "find out what everyone else is doing and then do the opposite."

If you choose to be different in some way, you cannot be very concerned with what other people think. You can't waste your energy worrying about what others will think about your beliefs and actions. Of course, you must do your research and homework first. But once you have decided, you have to trust yourself and your judgment more than you trust others, even if they are in the majority. That takes courage.

What if everyone were normal and average? Who would have the adventures? Who would invent new things? Who would make the advances in ideas and processes? Who would take the chances that lead to progress?

We need people who will dare to be different. These are the people who make the great breakthroughs.

You are special and unique. There is no one like you. If you choose to be just like everybody else, what will happen to your specialness and your uniqueness?

Be special, be unique, be you. Dare to be different.

QUESTIONS

1. In what ways do you deliberately conform to what others want you to be? For example, the clothes you wear might be conforming to the kinds of clothes your friends wear, your employer expects, the kinds of advertisements you read, among other things. Why did you choose the clothes you are now wearing?

2. Do you agree with the statement, "It doesn't take any talent just to go unthinkingly along with the crowd"? Why?

3. What are some advantages of conforming or going along with the crowd? What are some disadvantages?

4. Can you explain the relationship between being different, or thinking differently, and being creative?

5. Why do you suppose people who invent new machines and ideas are sometimes ridiculed, laughed at, or treated in other negative ways?

6. What happens to people in your group of friends who do not conform in some way? To what standards are your friends expected to conform and what treatment would they receive if they didn't conform? Would they be punished in some way or would they be praised? What would you do if the group ridiculed a member for not conforming to their informal dress code?

7. Are there any ways in which you and your group of friends conform to very strict norms in order to show the rest of society that you won't conform to the larger society's norms? What are they? For example, "My teenage friends and I always wear our clothes inside out to show we are different. If anyone in my group doesn't wear his clothes inside out, we make fun of him."

8. Have you ever known someone who seemed to make a profession out of being different (that is, someone who always tries to be different no matter what the situation just to draw attention to him/herself)? Do you see any problems for a person who acts in this way?

9. What do you mean by the term "normal" when you think of human behavior? Is not being normal good, bad, neutral, or something else? If something else, what?

ACTIVITIES

1. List reasons why we need "some people who dare to think differently and to act differently from the norm." Have everyone in your group share their reasons and make a master list.

2. Name some courageous acts that you have seen people your age perform (that is, times in which people, including yourself, did something they believed to be right even though it was different from what nearly everyone else was doing or saying should be done). These can be small things like picking up your trash at a picnic in the park when everyone else just leaves the trash on the tables for someone else to clean up. Share all of the courageous acts in your group and make a list of them. Which three would be the most difficult for you to do? Why? Share these in the group also.

3. Draw a picture or make a cartoon of someone being different from the crowd in a way that you think is courageous. Share it with others in the group. Do they understand it as you mean it?

4. Make a list of non-normal behaviors that you want to discourage (for example, people cheating other people in business transactions). Explain your list to others in your group. Have them explain theirs.

5. Make a list of atypical behaviors that you want to encourage (for example, people who volunteer to help others who are unable to help themselves). Explain your list to others in your group. Have them explain theirs.

6. Give two examples each of responsible differentness and irresponsible differentness.

7. What would the world be like if everyone conformed to an average? Describe your answer as though you observed this world through your own eyes. What would you see?

8. In your group of friends, there are certain things that are expected of you. Make a list of the things that are very clear and obvious. Make a list of those things that are expected but are seldom discussed. These are like unwritten laws of the group.

9. There is no one like you in this world. You are unique and special. What are some of the qualities and talents that you possess? You probably have many more qualities and talents that you can't think of right now. What you do with these qualities and talents will be your difference to this world.

CHAPTER 30

Spectators Don't Win Trophies

You are going to be a happier person if you are both a participant and a producer. This hypothesis, stated another way, is that you cannot be a fully-functioning human being if you are only a spectator and a consumer. You are going to get more out of your life when you get more directly involved in your life. Good mental health is better gained and sustained when you are a participant rather than a spectator. In the long run, you are going to have more fun in your life if you are a creator and a producer rather than only a consumer and a watcher. At this point in your life are you more a doer or a watcher?

Spectators can't win trophies. You can't just be a spectator and expect to make progress and have successes in your life. You have to be actively involved to win a trophy or attain any goals. Have you ever seen a winner of anything who was only a spectator? *Do it rather than just read about it.*

Being a spectator and a consumer are types of participation, but they are not of the same quality of participation as producing and creating. You will get a greater thrill if you create a ceramic vase than if you simply buy it. You are more likely to have a peak experience when you create a stained glass window than when you just look at it. You will find it more fulfilling to write a poem or short story than just to read it.

You get more of a feeling of accomplishment from being a participant than you do from being a watcher. Although millions of people have experienced awe when they viewed the Sistine Chapel, only Michelangelo and those who worked for him experienced the feelings of accomplishment and satisfaction that came from its creation. In everyday life, you and I find more accomplishment when we do things ourselves rather than hire someone to do them. Even simple things, like repairing something in your home, give far more satisfaction than having someone else do them while you watch. It is better not be perfect than it is just to be an observer.

Fear of failure, especially if we think someone is looking and judging us, stops many of us from participating. What we tend to forget is that everybody who ever became good at anything had to fail sometimes. *Nobody starts anything as an expert.* Olympic gold medal winners were awkward and inept the first time they tried their sports. The same is true of doctors, teachers, plumbers, and artisans of all types. Every expert at anything has had to overcome the fear of being ridiculed. The worst thing about the fear of failure is that it leads to the biggest failure of all—the failure to try. And participants usually burn more calories than spectators do!

Participants tend to be in better shape than spectators. If you are a participant, you have to use your body and your brain more than if you were only a spectator. Both your physical and mental muscles need to be exercised to keep in shape. They both tend to atrophy if they aren't used. If you don't believe this statement, check out the muscle tone and the mental tone of people who spend a lot of their lives just sitting around watching television or playing with their smart phones.

It is better to participate in sports than it is to watch them. I suggest that it is much better for you to play sandlot baseball with the neighborhood kids than it is to watch the World Series. I suggest it is much better for you to play a game of touch football in the backyard with friends and family than it is to watch the Super Bowl. I suggest that it is much better for you to play a mediocre game of golf than it is to watch the U.S. Open. I suggest that it is better for two hackers to play tennis than it is for them to watch Wimbledon. Karl Marx said that religion is the opium of the people. I suggest that today we might change that to spectator sports are the opium of the people. Perhaps we should all make a vow that we will spend at least as many hours participating in sports as we spend watching them.

Couch potatoes can't gain confidence. The only way you can gain confidence in yourself is by your accomplishments. You can't accomplish anything unless you participate in something. If you are only a spectator, how will you ever gain confidence in yourself? The best way to learn something and understand it is to *do* it.

What kind of self-image will people have if they don't participate and produce? How we see ourselves determines to a large extent how we behave. If we see ourselves as inept, we increase the likelihood that we will be inept. If we see ourselves as highly competent, we are more likely to be competent. What kind of self-concepts will people have if they only watch? Will they see themselves as only observers and consumers?

Will they see themselves as only blanks?

QUESTIONS

1. Do you believe it is true that your life will be better if you are an active participant as well as a spectator? Why or why not?

2. What is an activity that you have always wanted to do? Why don't you do it? List the reasons. What could you do to overcome these reasons? Are the reasons the kind that you cannot overcome or are they seen by you as too much trouble or too difficult to overcome?

3. What do you think of the idea that everyone should make a rule in his or her life that as much time will be spent participating and producing as will be spent observing and consuming?

4. If you call someone a couch potato, do you mean it to be negative? Explain.

5. Your self-image is how you see yourself. To what extent do you see yourself as a competent and confident person who is capable of meeting most challenges you will have in life? To what extent do you think your vision of yourself might be influenced by whether you are a participant/producer most of the time or whether you are a watcher/spectator most of the time?

ACTIVITIES

1. Over a period of time (choose a time from two days to a week or more), keep a record of the times that you are a spectator and the times that you are a participant. First, you need to decide how you will define these two terms. This record should be a description of what you do in your discretionary or free time. When you have a choice of what you do with your time, to what extent do you spend it on activities in which you participate or produce, and to what extent do you spend your time on activities in which you primarily watch or consume? This would not include eating, sleeping, your job, or anything you *must* do. Look at your results. Do you spend more of your time watching or participating? Is it about the same amount of time? Do you do much more of one than the other? Is there anything that you think you should change based on the data you have gathered about yourself?

2. Choose one activity that you most like to watch. You really enjoy being a spectator of this activity or event. Have you ever tried the activity as a participant? If not, why don't you find a way in which you could be a direct participant? If you couldn't be a direct participant, maybe you could be an indirect participant. For example, you might like to watch movies or plays. Is there a group you could join in which you could be an actor in a local play? If you couldn't or wouldn't want to be an actor, maybe you could be a member of the stage crew. The idea is to

get involved in doing something instead of only in watching. Once you have decided what you want to be involved in, what is the next step you must take?

3. See if you can put into words how being a participant could be a better way of making you feel good about yourself than just being a spectator. What case can you make for being a spectator? Share your ideas with others. Do they agree with you or not? Do you think you should make any changes in your life as a result of doing this activity?

4. Make a list of reasons you believe people choose to be spectators rather than participants. For example, people are often afraid they will look foolish doing the activity because they can't do it well yet. Are any of these reasons why *you* choose not to participate in some activities?

5. Write a short paragraph or two about someone who wins a trophy for being a spectator. Does it seem absurd or does it make some sort of sense? Explain.

6. Below are some things that people do as consumers or spectators. What are some producer or participant counterparts that you could do?

- Eating food

- Watching a ball game

- Watching television

- Reading a book

- Watching a race

- Going to a play

- Listening to music

- Observing paintings in a museum

- Looking at beautiful photographs in a magazine

- Admiring the landscaping around a home

- Admiring a person who is in excellent physical condition

- Listening to someone give an interesting speech

- Admiring different kinds of crafts at a fair or crafts show

CHAPTER 31

Overgeneralizing: How to Make One Equal Millions

You hear the screech of brakes. You swerve your car. You barely avoid a collision. An elderly driver nearly hit you. Later, you angrily tell a friend about what terrible drivers those old folks are. You don't mention the thousands of elderly people who are excellent drivers. You have overgeneralized one event involving one person to make a statement that includes many millions of people. You made the mental leap of one equals one million plus. We humans do a lot of this kind of overgeneralizing. We all have this tendency to draw hasty conclusions from too few facts. It's easy. This simple but common detriment to clear thinking and rational behavior can be seen in many parts of our lives. The following are descriptions of ways in which we often overgeneralize to the detriment of the clear thinking of ourselves and those around us.

Stereotyping is overgeneralizing about people. It occurs when someone believes the members of a group all have the same characteristics (for example, that all people on welfare are lazy). Stereotyping can be applied to any group. The following is a small sample of groups that are stereotyped. Take the time to complete each sentence with common stereotypes. How many can you name?

Politicians are...

Schoolteachers are...

Boy Scouts are...

People with red hair are...

Used car salesmen are...

Frenchmen are...

Catholics are...

Lawyers are...

African Americans are...

Mexicans are...

Fat people are...

Auto mechanics are...

Smokers are...

What other groups can you think of that are commonly stereotyped? Do you consider yourself part of any groups that have stereotypes applied to them? How are such generalizations unfair?

Now refer to the list of groups above. What can you say about these groups that is a true description about all the people in that group? It is very difficult to make an observation or description that validly includes all of the individuals in any group.

Prejudice is another form of overgeneralization.
Prejudice means prejudging someone or some group, usually in a negative way. That prejudgment is a belief about the person or group. The belief is usually a stereotype. Prejudice is the act of *pre-judging* people before you really know them. For example, if you believed the stereotype that automobile mechanics are all dishonest and you met a person who identified herself as a mechanic, you automatically would prejudge her to be dishonest even before you knew her well enough to know how honest she really is.

Note that it is not prejudice or overgeneralization if you have been cheated by a mechanic several times and then conclude that this mechanic is dishonest in her dealings with you. It would be an overgeneralization to say the mechanic was a dishonest person, however. You can only truly say the mechanic was dishonest in her dealings with you. She may be very honest with other customers, her friends, and her family. Valid generalizations do not go beyond the facts.

The mass media can lead us to overgeneralize.
Many of our beliefs now come through mass media such as television, radio, the internet, music, movies, magazines, and newspapers. The writers and performers who produce these media have beliefs that they express through their art. You and I watch, listen to, and read these media. We often accept the beliefs expressed in them to be true and normal. This is another way that we overgeneralize.

For example, if you watch a situation comedy on television for a season or two, you have a tendency to accept many of the behaviors and beliefs represented on that show as true and normal. If the show depicts a Mexican family in which parents and children are constantly in conflict, you will have the tendency to overgeneralize that it is true and normal for Mexican families to be in conflict. You might overgeneralize even further that it is true and normal that families in general are in constant conflict.

Repetition can lead us to generalize that the thing being repeated is true and normal. If you watch television shows in which the characters are always drinking beer and smoking cigars, you are likely to believe that is normal behavior. Our minds record events that are not real in the same way that real events are recorded. This allows us to overgeneralize about the real world, using fictitious information that we see, hear, or read. The child who lives in a family in which the favorite entertainment is watching violent television shows is much more likely to believe that it is normal for problems to be solved through resorting to violence. Viewing violence, even if it is fictional violence, often leads to the overgeneralization that in real life it is normal (even heroic) for disputes to be settled by violence without attempting nonviolent means first.

The reporting of the news is a special concern. The news media evidently have determined that the news they are most likely to feature are events that are unusual. The more abnormal and bizarre an event is, the more newsworthy it seems to become. It is not news to report that millions of people got to work safely, did not break any laws, and enjoyed good health. It is news to show people who are badly hurt in a terrible car wreck, who are brutally beaten, or who get rare illnesses. In fact, news reports, especially local news, usually consist of murders, rapes, wars, accidents, conflicts, and disasters of all types. After years of watching on television and the Internet the worst and most bizarre human events that happen each day, we are quite likely to overgeneralize that this is the way the world truly is and that this is normal. Most of what is shown as news gives us a warped and negative view of the society in which we live. *Is it any wonder that so many of us have negative views about our country and our future when our society is depicted at its worst on the news every night?*

The reporting of sports on television offers a vivid illustration of the biased view of reality that is given to us by the media. Nearly all the news about sports is devoted to the most spectacular plays, fights, odd fans, disputes, or other unusual situations. If you only watched this kind of news to know the reality of sports, you would have a very unrealistic view of them. When only the unusual is stressed, we tend to overgeneralize and believe it to be true and normal. Sports are not a crucial part of our lives, but they can afford some obvious examples of ways in which unrealistic perspectives can be obtained through the mass media.

We even overgeneralize about ourselves. You and I are very complex creatures. We have many talents. We can do thousands of tasks. We are far more intricate than the most powerful computers. We have thousands of images about ourselves as being capable of everything from playing softball to solving math problems. How do you see yourself as a tennis player? A mountain climber? A public speaker? A tooth brusher? A friend? A singer? If you listed all the roles you play in life and then added up all the self-images you have of yourself as a performer of those roles, you would have your overall self-esteem.

See what often happens when you do poorly in one of these roles, however. Let us imagine that you are a person with overall high self-esteem. You feel good about yourself and your place in the world. You feel confident that, if given enough time, you can accomplish just about anything that you feel is worthwhile doing. You are happy and enjoying your life.

You go out to play golf for relaxation. Your image of yourself as a golf player is good, but today you have a terrible game. Everything you do goes wrong. You end the day with your worst golf score in years. Now, how will you think about that golf score and yourself? You should tell yourself that you know you are a good golfer and a good person who had one bad day shooting golf, but you enjoyed the outdoors and are relaxed and happy; however, you could overgeneralize by thinking that your one bad day of shooting golf makes you unhappy, a bad golfer, and a generally less worthy person.

Your negative thinking starts with a negative experience in golf, which is overgeneralized to a negative self-image as a golfer, which is then overgeneralized to a less positive total self. Although it sounds ridiculous when explained, it is something that every one of us has done at some time or another. One bad experience does not make you a bad person.

We often overgeneralize negative feedback. Have you ever seen a little child come home from school and tearfully announce that nobody at school likes him? After some careful questioning it is discovered that one of the other children at school laughed when he gave a wrong answer. The one negative action by one person was overgeneralized to mean that all of the children and faculty at the school dislike him. Again, this might seem like a childish thing to do, but we adults often do the same thing. An employee who gets constructive criticism on a periodic evaluation can overgeneralize that the supervisors all hate her and that she is incompetent. The college student who receives a low grade can overgeneralize that the professors do not like him, are out to get him, and that he is stupid. Have you ever overgeneralized the negative feedback you have gotten?

What can you do to prevent overgeneralizing?

Ask yourself if you have enough data to warrant your conclusion logically. Can I make this statement based on what I know? Would others logically come to the same conclusion if they knew what I know? Would I come to the same conclusion if I knew more?

Be aware of using (thinking) terms that are all-inclusive. Be wary of using words such as all, always, and never. Do all redheads have quick tempers? Are Frenchmen always great lovers? Does your friend never give you a compliment?

Use qualifiers in your speech and your thinking. Use words such as some, many, a majority, most, probably, and other terms that indicate that you are thinking in more precise tenets. Be as specific as possible, but if you are not sure of exact figures, use these or similar qualifiers to avoid overgeneralizing.

Think of people as individuals, not as members of a group. It is seldom helpful to think of individuals as members of a group. Can you think of an instance in which it is more useful to think of a person as a member of a group rather than as an individual? I personally want people to treat me as an individual and not as a member of some bogus group term such as American, Caucasian, professor, or middle-aged. Groups are composed of individuals but few, if any, individuals represent all the characteristics that are attributed to any group. Can you think of any situation in which you would rather be thought of as a member of a group than as an individual?

Treat others as you would like to be treated. Several years ago there was a fad in which people told jokes about blonde women. These blonde jokes were all based on the stereotype that blondes were not very smart. The jokes perpetuated this stereotype, even though there was no truth to it. Very few of us would like to have jokes made about our supposed lack of intelligence. If we would find it uncomfortable to be labeled or stereotyped in this way, we should not label or stereotype others. The Golden Rule makes sense.

Perhaps you should consider simply not using labels or groupings in your thought or conversations. Group nouns such as conservatives, Jews, westerners, teenagers, parents, women, and whites are imprecise labels that are so easily overgeneralized that they should probably not be used in our thinking or conversation. Although this may seem very radical, can you think of any real-life situations in which the use of terms such as these would describe reality and lead to clearer thinking than thinking in terms of individuals?

Constantly monitor your thinking and language as well as the language of others for overgeneralizations. Don't allow yourself or others to overgeneralize.

It won't be easy, but it will be worth it.

QUESTIONS

1. What is the difference between a valid generalization and an overgeneralization? Give at least one original example of each.

2. What do you think is the best thing to do when someone you know makes a prejudicial statement? Give an example of a situation and how you would react.

3. Can you give an original example of the idea that "repetition can lead you to overgeneralize that the thing being repeated is true and normal"?

4. Some people describe overgeneralizing as being the same as "jumping to a conclusion before you have enough facts." Which do you think is a better description?

5. Can you remember situations in which you overgeneralized about someone?

6. Can you remember situations in which you overgeneralized about yourself?

7. Do you agree with the statement that we should not use labels or groupings of people (for example, Chinese, high school students, and so on) in our thinking and conversations? Why or why not?

8. If you didn't use labels or group nouns for people because they are too imprecise, what would you use? How would you describe people? For example, what would be a more precise way of describing people we usually call conservatives, Jews, radicals?

9. Choose some labels that are used by you and your friends and see whether you can describe them in precise ways rather than as imprecise group nouns.

10. Do you know a joke that stereotypes? Why is the joke considered funny? What is the stereotype? Do you think the humor is worth what the stereotype teaches? Do you know of any jokes that are told about groups to which you belong?

ACTIVITIES

1. Describe a fictional person for whom you choose gender, skin color, shade, religion, nationality, age, and job. Then write down the common stereotypes that might be attributed to that person by someone who uses stereotypes. If you are meeting with a group, share your individual fictional stereotypes among yourselves. How is this stereotyping of fictional characters different from stereotyping of real people? How is it similar?

2. Complete the categories or groupings in the preceding activity for yourself. To what common stereotypes would you be subjected? If you are meeting in a group, have other people add stereotypes to your personal profile. Now analyze the stereotypes. Do any seem to be correct and fair? Which are not correct? Did you learn anything about stereotyping from this activity? If so, share it with the total group.

3. Have you ever been pre-judged by someone? Describe briefly what happened. If you are meeting in a group, have each person share what happened when he or she was the object of another person's prejudice.

4. Discuss and make a list of how a person can guard against being prejudiced against someone.

5. As an individual or in a group, list the stereotypes you might have of the United States if you watched only a

certain program on television. You choose which program. For example, if you chose a program about police officers who catch criminals, you might stereotype the United States as a place in which nearly everyone was a criminal or a police officer and that the police officers always caught the criminals.

6. Choose one show on television that you watch regularly. Pretend that you are a creature from another world and that you watch this show regularly. It is the only show you see. Based on what you would see repeated each week, what generalizations would you be likely to make? Would these be true generalizations about the United States? Would they be generalizations or overgeneralizations? Discuss how this is different from your watching that show each week.

7. Watch some regular local television newscasts. What generalizations could be made about the United States or your state if you only used the television newscasts as your source of facts? When you have made your list of generalizations, discuss whether or not they are real based on your experience. That is, are the things reported on the news a good sample of what really happens in our society?

8. Write a short description of a situation in which a person overgeneralizes. Make it a funny story if you can. Have the person jump to a conclusion that is ridiculous and silly.

9. Illustrate an overgeneralization by drawing a cartoon or picture, constructing a collage, or using other visual media.

CHAPTER 32

Quality Questions and a Quality Life

Questions are wonderful. We need to ask lots of questions. They get us to think. They can cause us to see things we never saw before. They can uncover new ways of seeing things. They can focus our energy. They can be excellent planning tools. Questions can stir us out of our mental and habitual ruts. Asking provocative questions is an important part of living a productive, stimulating, and happy life. If you are one of those who says you are too busy just existing to take the time to ask important questions, you might be missing a stimulating experience and a major opportunity to improve the quality of your life.

Most of the questions below concern beliefs. Our beliefs determine our behavior. That is, we hold many beliefs and we usually act consistently with those beliefs. Many of the questions in this chapter are important because they are about crucial beliefs, which then become crucial behaviors in our lives as individuals and as members of our society.

I suggest that you might read through the questions and mark those that strike you as most important at this point in your life. Then choose the one that seems the most important.

Sit down by yourself and think it through. Better yet, take the time to put your answer down in writing. Decide where you stand. Perhaps you want to make it part of a discussion with a person who is close to you. Perhaps there are some questions that would be most appropriate for family discussions. Be sure to develop your own questions. The main purpose is to choose a question that is important to you and think it through. Here are some of the questions that I have found important.

- What is my purpose or mission in life?

- What does it mean to act morally?

- What are the five (5) most important possessions I have?

- Do I practice what I advocate?

- Do I treat others as I would like them to treat me?

- Am I primarily a participator or a spectator?

- Would I like to live with someone like me?

- What things have I always wanted to do in my life but haven't? Why am I not doing those things now? Which one will I start now?

- Do I really need a lot of money to be happy?

- Do I have some habits that I know are not good for me? Why do I continue them? Why don't I change these habits now?

- Do I know of some habits that I should have but don't? Why do I not start one of these habits now?

- What are the things that make me really happy? How can I arrange my life to do these things more often?

- Can I incorporate things that I love to do into my vocation?

- What things could I do now to make my present work more interesting and enjoyable?

- When will I be old? Do I ever have to be old or do I just get older?

- Is there anything that isn't best done in moderation?

- What are the most important qualities I admire in others? Do I have those qualities myself? If not, should I acquire them?

- Have I recently told those I love how much they mean to me?

- Do I consistently look at the positive in my life rather than dwell on what I interpret as negative?

- Have I complimented someone close to me lately?

- Have I complimented myself recently?

- What could I do today just for the fun of it?

- Do I consistently forgive and forget unpleasant things done to me?

- Do I really have to do all the things that I think I have to do?

- Do I usually look for the good in people and events, or do I usually look for the bad in people and events?

- For what would I be willing to give up my dignity, pride, honor, or integrity?

- What is beauty and should I get more of it in my life?

- Would I ever be justified in hitting a child or in killing someone?

- Would I ever be justified in hating, cheating, lying, stealing, gossiping, or making fun of someone in a way that hurts him?

- Do I consistently ask "why" questions before I ask "how" questions?

- Do I firmly, but diplomatically, stand up for what I think is right?

- What is the best use of the time I have left in my life?

What other questions should you ask?

QUESTIONS

1. Which of the questions on the list are most important to you at this time in your life?

2. Which questions make you uncomfortable? Can you figure out why they make you uncomfortable?

3. Are there other questions which are more important to you now? What are they?

4. Which are the easiest questions for you to address? Why?

5. Do you think very often about the kinds of things that these questions make you think about? If you don't think very often about these aspects of life, why do you suppose that you don't?

ACTIVITIES

1. With a partner or a small group of two to three, compare the questions each of you has chosen as the most important. Take turns to explain why the questions are important to you at this time in your life.

2. Go through the list of questions in the chapter and choose the five that you would want the president of the United States to answer. Do the same for some other person or group such as a parent, a close friend, the state legislature, or your family. Construct your own questions for these people and groups that will get them to think about what is important.

3. Write down the questions from the list that you think your parents or guardians would want you to answer. Do the same for the questions a concerned teacher, a close friend, or anyone else would want you to address.

CHAPTER 33

Standing Up for What You Believe Is Right

How do you react when someone does something mean to you? What do you do when someone does something dishonest to you? What do you do when someone treats you unfairly? Your reactions to situations like these can determine how others will treat you in the future and, perhaps more importantly, how good you feel about yourself.

We usually have one of three different reactions when we are confronted with what we feel is an unfair situation. The most common reaction is to do nothing, say nothing, and submissively accept the unfair situation even though it makes us feel unhappy, upset, or angry. The second kind of reaction to an unfair situation is to get angry, attack, and be aggressive. Another kind of response to an unfair situation is to assert calmly, diplomatically, and sincerely how the situation is unfair and what should be done to make it fair. Each of these common responses has consequences that should be considered. This chapter is about the different responses and their probable consequences.

Submissive/Passive Responses

You have been standing in line for 10 minutes. You are now near the front of the line when a person you have never seen before steps in front of you. You are angry. You want to tell him to get to the end of the line just like everyone else, but you don't say anything. You don't do anything. You don't know what to do, but you want to do something. Before you think of what to do, he has finished his business and leaves. For a long time afterward, you think of what you should have said and what you should have done. You become angry with yourself for letting someone take advantage of you. You berate yourself for your inaction, submissiveness, and meekness. You mentally label yourself as a submissive wimp and say goodbye to a big chunk of your self-esteem.

As implied in the preceding example, there are many reasons why being submissive is undesirable. Some of the main reasons are:

- ***You teach the person or institution that treated you unfairly that they can continue to treat you unfairly, and you probably won't do anything about it.*** Your inaction actually reinforces the unfair action and increases the probability that it will happen again. For example, if the man who cut in front of you in line is in a hurry again and sees you standing in a line, chances are good that he will cut in front of you again.

- ***You lose some control of your life.*** When you are submissive and don't want to be, you have lost some control of your life. You have given a big chunk of control of your life to the person you allowed to take advantage of you.

318

• *You lose some self-esteem.* You don't like yourself as much when you don't do something that you feel you should have done.

• *You might feel guilty.* This guilt surfaces because you acted inconsistently with your conviction that you should stand up for what you believe is right.

• *You feel like a slave.* Slaves must be subservient and submissive to a person or institution; you are in many ways a slave in that relationship.

There are, however, some instances when being submissive is the proper choice of alternatives. For example, you may choose to act submissively because you know that you are dealing with an irrational person. You may choose to behave submissively in the short run to give you time to think of better responses in the long run. If the man who cuts in front of you in line is obviously the member of a gang (other gang members are standing nearby) that has a reputation for violence, and there are no law enforcement officers around, it would be very wise to act submissively. In this kind of situation, you make a choice that is not desirable but is the least undesirable of the choices available. This is not being a wimp. This is controlling your life by making a rational decision to be submissive for a very valid reason.

Most times, however, being submissive and passive is a habit of responding that not only allows and teaches others to treat us unfairly but also robs us of self-esteem and dignity.

Aggressive/Attack Responses

You have driven to a store across town to purchase an item. You buy the item and take it back across town to your home only to find that some of the parts are missing. You are upset. Now you must drive back across town. When you arrive at the store, you angrily confront the clerk. You tell her how much of an inconvenience this was to you, how incompetent the manufacturer is, and how lousy her store is. You further attack the clerk and threaten to have her fired if she doesn't get your money back immediately. Other customers and clerks detour around you as they watch your maniacal outburst. You have just illustrated an aggressive or attack response.

Some people make it a habit to respond aggressively to everything they perceive as an injustice. They imitate Attila the Hun by responding with a knee-jerk attack on whomever or whatever they perceive as being unfair to them. Their outbursts are often followed by feelings of guilt for having attacked an innocent person such as the clerk in the above example. There is often a feeling of having acted stupidly without thinking. There are also often physiological responses such as tenseness, stomach upsets, and headaches that result from these outbursts.

There is a relationship between submissive and aggressive responses that is very important. It can explain what might seem to be bizarre behavior. Many times a person, who is usually submissive and meek, will suddenly and unexpectedly explode and be very aggressive. For example, a husband may be in the habit of leaving a mess around his favorite chair in which he reads every night. His wife is irritated by this habit because she picks up after him, but she submissively lets it pass year after year. Each time she cleans his mess, however, it makes her angry at her husband for being so sloppy and inconsiderate, and she is angry at herself for allowing her husband to treat her in such an unfair way. This anger builds up for years. Finally, one day, she has had enough and as her husband gets up from his crumb-strewn, paper-littered, coffee-stained chair, the pent-up anger explodes. She attacks him as having the manners of a Neanderthal and the consideration of a worm. The startled husband honestly does not know what is happening and feels he is being assaulted for no apparent reason by a wife who has suddenly gone mad. He was just behaving like he has for years and, without warning, he was attacked as if he had committed some terrible crime.

This unfortunate situation could have been averted if the wife had dealt with her husband's sloppy behavior when it started. Instead, her long-term submissiveness resulted in a slow build-up of anger and frustration that unexpectedly erupted in an aggressive attack that her husband did not understand.

Aggressive responses seldom gain anything positive. Aggression usually begets more aggression. If the aggression causes submission, the submissive person usually becomes an enemy. If submissive and aggressive responses have such limited positive use, what is the preferable way to respond to a situation in which you feel you are treated unfairly?

Diplomatic-Assertive Responses

You have just been served your meal in the restaurant. You take your first bite and discover that the food is cold. You like it hot. You get the waiter's attention. With a smile you inform him that you understand he is not at fault, but your food is cold and you would appreciate it if he would warm it up for you. You could have passively and submissively eaten the cold food and not enjoyed the meal you paid for. Many people behave that way each day. Or you could have aggressively attacked the waiter as being incompetent and inconsiderate. Many people do that each day. Instead, you have chosen to explain to the waiter what is wrong and what positive action would make it right. You acted in a kind and considerate manner, which allowed the waiter to keep his dignity. But you made it clear that you were not satisfied, explained the reason for your dissatisfaction, and communicated what would make you satisfied. You were diplomatic and assertive. You made it clear what you believed was fair and just, but you did it in a way that preserved the dignity of all involved.

Advantages of the diplomatic-assertive approach:

- You will teach the people who treated you unjustly that you will not tolerate injustice. You are a stronger person than they perhaps expected you to be when they treated you unfairly.

- You express your position in specific terms. Others know exactly what you feel is unfair and exactly what you think needs to be done to make it fair. Too often, people appear to be angry or upset about something without being clear about what is wrong or what needs to be changed to make them happier.

- Your diplomatic approach saves others' dignity and it can save you a lot of enemies.

- You can feel good about yourself because you have shown the courage to stand up for what you believe is right. Most people do not speak up for what they believe is right. It has been estimated that about 80 percent of the time, we respond to unfair situations in submissive ways.

- Even if your diplomatic-assertive response does not get you the fairness that you desire, you can be proud of yourself for being among the few who promote justice.

- You will improve your self-concept. You have to feel proud of yourself when you show strength of character in a negative situation.

- You are contributing to the cause of justice and fairness in society as a whole.

- You are acting as a model of a rational and positive response to what you perceive as unjust or unfair. Others will see your behavior and can use it as a guide to their behavior.

Important characteristics of successful diplomatic-assertive responses:

- Be polite. Preserve others' dignity as well as your own.

- Be calm. Keep your cool even if the situation angers you.

- Precisely state what is unfair and how it makes you feel.

- Precisely state what needs to be done to stop what you perceive as the injustice.

- Describe; don't attack, don't accuse, and don't whine.

- Don't wait. Be assertive as soon as you feel unjustly treated.

- Act as if everyone is rational. You will usually be correct.

You might allow for misinterpretation by starting with qualifiers such as, "Perhaps I am not seeing this correctly, but…" or, "I want to check a perception…" or, "Help me understand….." Opening phrases of this kind soften the tone of the conversation and make it less likely to be seen as an accusation.

In summary, when confronted with a situation that you feel is unjust, unfair, or in some other way undesirable, you have at least three choices. You can choose the extremes of acting either submissively or aggressively.

Or you can choose an approach of tactfully asserting what you believe is right and just.

The choice is yours!

QUESTIONS

1. Many people get assertive and aggressive behavior confused. How would you explain the difference between these two ways of responding to what you feel is unfair? Answer as if you were talking to someone who had never heard of the terms.

2. When you are being assertive, you want to preserve the dignity of the person to whom you are being assertive. What do you mean when you use the word "dignity"?

3. It has been said that doing something or saying something that takes away someone's dignity also gains you an enemy. Do you believe that? Have you ever had an experience that would illustrate your position?

4. Can you explain how being assertive could make you feel good about yourself and improve your self-esteem?

5. Some people say that being assertive takes courage. Do you agree or not? Why?

6. Why is it that people who allow themselves to consistently behave submissively are often looked upon in a negative way by others? Why would it be that people who habitually act submissively feel negatively about themselves?

7. In your own words, define what you think an assertive person does. How does the assertive person act? You might want to list the characteristics of the behavior of the assertive person.

8. You can choose to act submissively, aggressively, or assertively when you feel you have been treated unjustly or unfairly. What do you mean when you use the words "unjust" or "unfair" when you describe people's treatment toward you?

ACTIVITIES

1. Think of a time in your life when you were submissive in a situation when someone did something that you felt was unfair. Write down how you felt at that time. Did you feel proud of yourself? Do you agree with the reasons listed in the chapter explaining why being submissive is undesirable? Can you add any reasons? Do you disagree with any of the reasons? Why?

2. Write out an original situation that is a good example of appropriately choosing to behave submissively in the short term because of unusual circumstances. Explain how being submissive in your particular situation would be a wise choice and not just an easy choice. If you are meeting with a group, share your situations and discuss how well the situations illustrate good short-term uses of submissive behavior.

3. Describe a situation in your life in which you acted submissively for a time about something and let your frustration build up until you finally lashed out angrily and aggressively. What could you have done assertively that would have lessened the possibility of your final blow-up? If you didn't have a real-life situation like this happen to you, can you create one that would be a good example?

4. Think about the television shows that you watch. Which of the three ways of behaving (submissive, aggressive, or assertive) is the most used by the characters? Why do

you suppose the makers of the television shows use that way the most? What does that teach people who watch the shows about dealing with situations that they feel are unfair?

5. Pretend you are watching a movie that you have looked forward to seeing for a long time. You are enjoying it very much until a family sits in the row behind you. The mother and father let their little boy talk out loud, make noise by shaking the ice in his drink, kick the back of your seat, and even throw popcorn into your row. You try to ignore the child but are constantly distracted by his behavior. It is obvious the parents are not going to do anything to make the child stop his annoying behaviors. Write out how you would act if you responded (a) submissively, (b) aggressively, and (c) assertively. If you are meeting in a group, share your answers. Help each other to be sure that the examples are good ones. Based on others' feedback, modify your answers to make them better examples. Which way of behaving was the easiest to describe? Which was the most difficult to describe? Which is actually the most difficult to do?

6. Develop your own situation like the one immediately above. Perhaps you can base it on a real experience, or you might want to create your own fictitious situation. Write it out on a piece of paper. If you are meeting with a group, put each of your situations in a box and draw one out and read it to the group. Then have people count off by threes. Have one group write out how they would respond to the situation being submissive, another

aggressive, and the other assertive. Be sure to share the products and to critique them for their accuracy of describing that kind of behavior.

CHAPTER 34

Friends, Relationships, and the Golden Rule

Everybody wants to have friends. We like the company of other people. We like to be recognized by others. We like to feel that we belong. We like to have someone with whom we can talk in confidence. We like the security of knowing there are people we can count on when we need them. But why do some of us have few friends while some of us have many friends? Why do some people have harmonious relationships for many years while others have a difficult time even establishing a positive relationship?

We can explore ideas about the ways in which people establish and maintain positive relationships. Positive, friendly, harmonious relationships can be with anyone; however, you certainly want to have friendly, positive relationships with those close to you, such as a spouse, parents, children, and relatives. You might think it is odd to say that your spouse should be a friend. In fact, it might be a good idea to marry a friend rather than someone with whom you are romantically in love. Love is often a physical attraction or a short-term infatuation, while friendship can be more long-lasting. Ideally, shouldn't your spouse also be your best friend?

Friendships would also include those with whom you work, play, and otherwise have some regular contact. Think about each of the ideas presented here. Is it how you would like others to treat you? Is it the way that you normally treat others? Is it a way that you should treat others? Here are some suggestions showing how you can start and strengthen relationships.

- *In general, treat others as you would like to be treated. Whether they are religious or not, nearly everyone agrees with the Golden Rule.* It is easy to remember, and it is almost always correct when it is applied within the same cultural or ethnic group. If something hurts you when someone does it to you, then you shouldn't do it to anyone else. Wouldn't our relationships and the world be a lot more harmonious if we all treated each other as we would like to be treated?

- *Look for the good in others.* It is very easy to fall into the trap of looking for the bad things people do. This is especially true of those who are close to us. We often take their many positive attributes for granted and focus on their few faults. Make it a personal habit to look deliberately for the good in others such as manners, looks, habits, grooming, work, and so on. Wouldn't you prefer that people emphasize your assets rather than your liabilities? Accentuate the positives in life.

- *Compliment others on the good things you see in them.* If you are looking for the positives in others, you are more likely to find positives. When you see them doing something praiseworthy, be sure to praise that behavior. Let them know that you recognize their excellent qualities. Let them know that you appreciate their contributions. Recognition doesn't need to be much. An honest word of praise, a pat on the back, or a short complimentary note is often enough. Even small recognitions like these strengthen relationships. They are especially valuable because they emphasize the positive, build self-esteem, and provide motivation for further accomplishments.

• ***Help others meet their needs and achieve their goals.*** When you help others achieve their desires, they see you as a positive part of their lives. When you help others achieve their goals, you also are helping yourself. In fact, many people believe the best way to achieve your needs is to help others achieve their needs. Solid relationships are built on recognizing and contributing to the achievement of the needs and goals of others.

• ***When you help others, don't expect them to return your favors in kind.*** If you do someone a favor, don't expect a favor in return. If you volunteer some service, give a present, give a compliment, or in any other way do something positive for someone, do not expect them to reciprocate. If you expect something in return and don't get it, you will be disappointed, and it can hurt your relationship. Do things for others because you want to or because you believe it is right, not because you expect something in return.

• ***Talk about them rather than yourself.*** Be sure that any meetings or conversations are in large part about the others in your group rather than about you. Remember how frustrated you feel when others only want to talk about themselves? Remember how important you feel when others honestly show an interest in you and what you are doing? This does not mean that you never talk about yourself. It does mean that you want to give others some, if not most, of the attention. It is very easy to be excited about something in your life and want to talk about it while you forget that others need attention as much as, or perhaps even more than, you do.

- *Call others by their names every chance you get.* Using people's names shows that you care enough about them to remember them. It is a sign of value.

- *Smile at people when you meet them.* Smile and nod, even to strangers whom you casually meet on the street.

- *Greet people. Initiate the greeting. Say it with enthusiasm.* By acting enthusiastically, you are increasing the chances that you will actually be enthusiastic and that it will spread to the person you greeted. Maybe it won't always work, but it certainly has to be better than the glum, the-world-is-going-to-dump-on-us-again-all-day grumbles that we often encounter. Greet people with a statement that emphasizes the positive such as, "What a fantastic day!" Greet people as you would like to be greeted.

- *Use your sense of humor.* This doesn't mean that you memorize a joke each day and go around telling it to everybody (sometimes more than once to the same people) in the belief that this is a way to become popular. It also doesn't mean that you monopolize every conversation with your jokes and funny stories. It does mean that you should feel free to use your sense of humor, but you should use it judiciously and in good taste. Everyone likes a good laugh.

• *Touch.* This doesn't mean that you have to hug everyone or give a massage to everyone you meet. It does mean that, when it is natural, you can establish closer bonds with others if you make physical contact with them. A touch on the hand, arm, shoulder, or back are usually acceptable ways to fulfill this human need for physical contact. A casual hug can also work. This suggestion needs to be applied with great care, however, because some people, and particularly some cultures, can interpret physical touch to be something far different from what you mean. For this reason, it might be wise to refrain from touching during the initial stages of a relationship until you know that it will be accepted as you mean it.

• *Allow your friends to make mistakes.* You and I make mistakes and know they are natural and no big deal. We need to allow those close to us to make their own natural mistakes.

• *Always treat others with dignity.* We are all human beings and deserve to be treated with dignity, regardless of our stations in life. Wonderful relationships can be developed with people who are usually overlooked. Think of all the people who do things for us and with us every day but are seldom acknowledged. Do you recognize them and their contributions? Do you greet them with the same enthusiasm as you greet colleagues? Do you accord them the dignity they deserve regardless of their assigned work?

- *Be honest.* A positive relationship cannot be based on dishonesty. Dishonesty, when discovered, results in the loss of credibility. It is difficult to have a lasting relationship with someone you cannot trust. Honesty builds trust and trust builds solid relationships.

- *Ask for advice.* It is quite a compliment to others when you ask for their advice. It shows your confidence in them and in their expertise, problem-solving skills, or other relevant skills. You get advice, your advisor gets a compliment, and the relationship gets stronger based on these positive exchanges.

- *Don't gossip.* Even though many people like to hear gossip, it is probably true that no one really trusts a person who gossips. When others tell you gossip, don't you have trouble trusting them? Don't you suspect that if they are telling you about someone else, they are probably telling someone else about you? That is not the basis of a long and enduring relationship.

- *Be a good listener.* Good relationships are based on good communication. Good communication is a two-way process. You have to be a good receiver as well as a good sender. Friends sometimes need to talk through difficult times or share the joys in their lives. They can only do that if there is someone to listen— really listen. Perhaps really listening to what your friends have to say now will model the kind of listening you will want and need from them in the future.

- *Respect others' rights to be different.* Don't expect others to be like you or act like you want them to. We are all individuals and have our rights to our individuality. Share, celebrate, and learn from the differences among your friends and other relationships. These differences can add new ideas, variety, and spice to your life. Be wary of wanting everybody to be like you. If you want everybody to be like you, you will have to try to change the very people with whom you want to have your best relationships. Trying to change others, especially those close to us, is morally questionable and is a nearly impossible task. It is also an almost guaranteed way to lose friends and alienate people.

- *Be a positive person to be around.* We all like for those close to us to be positive and uplifting. We like to be around people who can raise our spirits when we feel low. We like to be around people who see the good in us, events, and in life in general. We do not like to be around people who are constantly griping, moaning, and groaning. These are the people we avoid. So look for the good in your life and emphasize the positive in your relationships. If you think about it, you have a lot of reasons to be justly proud, grateful, thankful, and positive.

- *Do little things that are not expected.* Don't wait until the holidays to do something nice for others near you. Do things like:

  - Send a card just for the fun of it

  - Make a phone call at an unusual time

  - Have some of their favorite flowers delivered

  - Give a book or magazine about one of your loved one's interests

- Give a recording that expresses your feelings

- Send a cartoon cut from the newspaper that reminds you of someone

- Invite someone for a quiet walk

The idea here is to use your imagination to do something unusual and unexpected that will let those in relationships with you know that you are thinking of them. Finally, remember how you choose to treat others is a good predictor of how they will treat you in return. This treatment of each other then determines the kind and quality of your relationships.

How you initiate that relationship will have a major influence on how that relationship will develop.

QUESTIONS

1. What do you mean when you use the word "friendship"? What do friends do to be friends?

2. What are some words that you would use to describe friendship? Examples are being a good listener, not talking about you behind your back, having a good sense of humor, and so on.

3. What do you think are the characteristics and behaviors that make you a good friend? That is, how do you think your friends would describe what makes you a good friend?

4. Are there any changes that you might like to make in your behavior that would probably make you a better friend or increase the quality of your relationships? What is keeping you from making those changes?

5. Do you need friends to be truly happy? Is there such a thing as being your own friend and enjoying your own company? Would it be best to have some friends but also enjoy those times when you are by yourself?

6. Some people seem to use television as a substitute for friends. Can television be a good substitute for friends? Why or why not?

7. Could you ever have too many friends?

8. What makes the difference between a friend and a really good friend?

9. Can you think of any situations in which it would not be good to treat others as you would like them to treat you?

10. What are some characteristics of a good listener? That is, how do you know that someone is listening to you? When you are listening to others, do you show those characteristics?

11. Have you ever been in a situation in which you should have told a friend something for his or her own good but didn't for some reason? Why didn't you tell the person, even though it would have been of help to him or her? Would you tell him or her now if it happened again?

ACTIVITIES

1. Make a list of things that people do to, for or with you that make you feel good. Examples are complimenting your clothes, praising your work, sending you a thank-you-note when you have done them a favor, etc. If you are in a group, share your lists and make a master list of things that make you all feel good. Keep a record of the number of times each is chosen. Which ones are most popular? Now that you have a list of the most popular things that make people happy, what does that say to you and to how you interact with other people?

2. Of all the suggestions for beginning and maintaining friendships listed, which five do you consider to be the most important? If you are in a group, compare your five with those of others. Have each person explain why his or her selections are important.

3. Describe how your ideal friend would act. Now think about how closely your behaviors are to that of your ideal friend.

4. Can you think of a situation in which a good friend would tell you something that you might not like to hear about yourself but might be good for you to know? If you are in a group, share your situations.

5. Discuss what you think gossip is. Why do you think people gossip? How do you feel about people who gossip a lot? Do you like to have people who gossip around you? Why? Why not?

6. Are there any suggestions in this with which you disagree? If so, why do you disagree? What would be a better thing to do?

7. Remembering that a friend could be a member of your family, plan something that you can do for one or more friends that they are not expecting. That is, it is not a holiday or time when they might expect a gift or consideration from you but you surprise them with something to let them know you are thinking about them and appreciate them.

8. What do you see as the advantages and disadvantages of having a friend who has the same beliefs, hobbies and interests as you? What would be the advantages and disadvantages of having a friend who has a lot of different beliefs, hobbies and interests than you? Share any insights you might have gotten from this activity.

9. Can you think of a personal experiment that would test the suggestion that "the ways you treat others will be a good predictor of how they will treat you"? Why not try it and see what happens?

CHAPTER 35

Separate the Idea from the Personality

An idea is a good one if it works for you regardless of who developed it. A good idea can come from anybody. A bad idea can come from anybody. Both good and bad ideas have come from the rich and the poor, from the educated and the uneducated, from kind people and from cruel people. Good ideas can come from people in prison and bad ideas can come from judges. There is simply no way to use either people's social standing or other categorizations to predict whether their ideas will consistently be good ones or bad ones.

Many people, however, will not listen to the ideas of someone or will not read what someone has written because of something undesirable they believe about that person. You have probably heard someone say, "I wouldn't read that. That author is_____." You can fill in the blank with an ethnic group, religious group, political group, a nationality, or any other kind of human categorization that would connote negativity on the part of the speaker.

A statement like this does not separate the idea from the person. It implies that a person in a certain category (this category is prejudged to be bad in some way) is incapable of thinking anything that might be valuable. Yet we know that useful ideas can come from anybody. This is simply another way of saying that prejudice can shut out excellent ideas. Fantastic ideas come from people who are not formally educated, who are not in the mainstream of society, who do not possess the physical characteristics that are currently held desirable by society, or who otherwise are deemed somehow undesirable by those who have prejudged them.

We can also err in the opposite direction. How many times do we accept the ideas of people who are well known or who fit in a human category that we judge to be good? An excellent example of this is the popular athlete who tells us that we should buy a certain product. Many people will buy a specific soft drink because a famous football player tells them they should. Similarly, movie stars are often asked whom to vote for or are asked other political questions about which they might have little information or even interest. Novelists, who deal in fiction, are asked about how they would deal with a national enemy as if they had expertise or interest in international politics or strategic warfare. Just because people are highly visible and famous does not mean they automatically have good ideas about everything.

Arguments or discussions are also situations in which ideas and personalities should be separated. In a situation in which there is a contest of ideas, the *ideas* should be the focus of the debate, and the *personalities* of the discussants should be kept out of it. For example, if a husband and wife were discussing whether the family should purchase a new car, the discussion should only be about the ideas that relate to the advisability of that purchase. It should deal with factual data that relate to ideas like needs, affordability, wants, priorities, and so on.

It sometimes happens, however, that the discussion is led away from the ideas and becomes more involved in the personalities of the people who are doing the discussing. This usually occurs when one of the discussants feels insecure about the lack of strength of the ideas in his or her argument and then attacks the personality of the other person.

For example, suppose the husband strongly desires a new car, but his wife objectively shows that this would be a foolish economic decision. Unable to dispute his wife's facts, the husband might try to shift the argument away from the facts, which are going against him, and use something negative about his wife to give strength to his argument. He might argue that his wife is from a family who never spends any money and that she is stingy. He claims that she never lets him have anything he wants. In this case the husband is introducing something about a person (his wife) instead of using ideas directly related to the discussion. His wife's family history of spending money has nothing to do with whether his family can afford a new car at this time. Even if his wife is stingy, it has nothing to do with whether the family can afford to purchase a new automobile. When extraneous personality data becomes part of the decision-making process, it decreases the probability that a good decision will result.

Distinguishing between ideas and personalities is both evident and important in a court of law. Judges have a primary responsibility to see that the cases before them are decided on the facts. They know involving the personalities of the participants can only lessen the probability that a good decision will be made. There are lawyers, however, who, upon sensing the case is going against them, will shift from arguing the facts to attacking the personality of the opposing lawyer or litigant. The judge must be able to detect this deception, stop it, and ask that it not be part of the evidence. Like these judges, you and I need to detect this kind of deception when it occurs in our lives.

Another good reason to keep ideas and personalities apart is to promote good human relations. This allows you to have a fight with ideas but still be friends with the person with whom you are arguing. You can have a strong disagreement about ideas but then go out to dinner with your opponent, who is still your friend. A person's disagreement with you should not make him your enemy. Perhaps you might think of the *ideas* as your enemies but their proponents as your friends or potential friends.

In summary, think of ideas as tools. You judge a tool for the way it will help you, not from whom you obtained it.

QUESTIONS

1. Have you ever felt that an idea of yours was not heard because of something about you that didn't have anything to do with your ideas? For example, as a young person, perhaps you wanted to tell an adult something you thought was important. The adult would not listen because "you are just a kid." Did anything like this ever happen to you? Maybe you weren't listened to because of something besides being too young. Maybe it was your skin color, religion, size, or some other category. How did it make you feel? What was lost in your situation?

2. Have you ever not paid attention to someone because of some idea that you had about him or her? For example, you didn't listen to the advice from an elderly neighbor because you didn't think that old people could have helpful ideas about today. Or perhaps you did not even converse with someone because you considered him to be suspicious because of his different skin color, religion, nationality, or something else.

3. Have you ever unquestioningly accepted information or an idea you assumed was correct because the person giving the information was in a perceived position of authority? For example, you buy a brand of soft drink because a musician you like says he drinks it in a television advertisement. Perhaps you unquestioningly accept your favorite sport star's ideas about dating, marriage, or politics. What was your experience of accepting an idea because it came from a famous person?

4. On what basis or bases should an idea be judged? One basis by which to judge an idea that is mentioned in this chapter is if it will work. Do you agree or disagree? Why? What other bases or criteria do you suggest?

5. What do you think of the idea that people should be able to have a good argument or disagreement about ideas but, when the argument is over, should be friends or at least not enemies? In other words, do you think it is possible or advisable to remain friends with someone even though you have disagreements with him or her? Do you think this should be applied to countries? Families? Religions? Can you think of any situations in which disagreeing on the *ideas level* but remaining friends on the *personal level* would not be the best approach?

ACTIVITIES

1. Create an original, realistic example of a situation in which someone won't listen to a good idea of another person. What is the idea? What reason is given that the person with the idea should be judged as not worthy to be heard? Is the reason the person won't listen to the idea a valid one? Why? It's your example, so make it a good one and make it a realistic one. If possible, share your example with others. Have them share their examples with you. Help each other by making suggestions showing how the examples might be made stronger. If you are in a group, list all of the ways your examples prejudged the speaker as not being worthy of being heard.

2. Make a list of all the unjust ways you or your group can think of that people could be categorized by others so that their ideas are disregarded on the *categorization* rather than on the *merit* of the idea. Examples: being too young, too old, a different nationality.

3. Make a list of unrealistic categories by which people could have their ideas unquestioningly accepted based on their popularity or some other positive characteristic which is not directly related to the idea. Examples would be a rock musician, movie star, or professional athlete.

4. Create an original example of a situation in which two people are having a discussion/disagreement about something. Describe their different positions. Then

describe how one of them perceives that the other person has a better argument. Now show how the person with the least power of ideas switches to attack the personality of the other person. Use an example that is realistic and would be understood by others with whom you share it. You might want to make this more interesting by using funny names or unusual situations, but be sure that it is a good example showing how an argument can be switched from the ideas to the personalities of the participants.

5. Do the last activity, but do it with others as a skit rather than in writing.

CHAPTER 36

What if You Believed You Were a Frog?

What if you did believe you were a frog? If you really believed you were a frog, you would act like a frog as much as you could. You probably wouldn't do a very good job because you don't know how frogs think, but you might hop around a bit, try to catch flies with your tongue, and look for other frogs with whom to make friends. The point is not about how well you can imitate a frog, but rather that the beliefs you have are very important parts of your life. Beliefs are so important because we human beings are programmed to act, as best we can, in ways that are consistent with what we believe. That is why you would act like a frog, as best you could, if you really believed you were a frog.

In other words, what you believe has a great influence on your actions. Every voluntary action you make is based on one or more beliefs that you have at that time. In turn, your actions have consequences to you, other people, and your environment. To make it easier to remember, you might think of this process as BAC (Beliefs lead to Actions that have Consequences). This could also be remembered as a formula: Beliefs + Actions = Consequences.

Of course, you don't believe that you are a frog, but you have other beliefs about yourself, your talents, other people,

351

other nations, health, morality, death, and so on. Beliefs such as these are very powerful and, to a large extent, drive your life. The following ideas explore the power of the beliefs we hold and some of the implications of how that power is acquired and used.

A belief is an idea that you hold to be true. It is a conviction that you believe about reality. A belief is an idea that expresses how you view the world. It is an expression of a value or values that you hold. Some examples of beliefs are:

- The earth is a spherical shape.

- I am an intelligent and industrious employee.

- People are about as happy as they make up their minds to be.

- I am responsible for my behavior and my happiness.

- It is wrong to cheat.

- Greed is the root of all evil.

- Everyone should be treated with dignity.

What are some of the specific beliefs that you now hold?

The more strongly you hold a belief, the more your actions will be consistent with that belief. For example, if you have the mild belief that you should treat others as you would want them to treat you, you might act that way with your friends, family, and others you already know; however, if you had a very strong belief that you should treat others the way you want to be treated, you would act that way with everyone. What are your most strongly held beliefs?

If someone can control your beliefs, he or she can control your behavior. Propaganda, advertising, and other attempts to control your behavior are based on first controlling your beliefs. Those who want you to buy something use many tricks to influence your beliefs. An obvious example is beer commercials that attempt to associate in your mind attractive people and having a good time with drinking beer. They want you to have a mental picture of yourself drinking beer and having a wonderful time with many attractive people. If you accept this mental picture as true, it can become a belief that you must have beer to have a good time with your friends.

Advertisers have programmed many people to believe exactly this. Of course, the advertisers do not show beer bellies, sick drunks, horrible auto accidents caused by drunk drivers, or any of the other negative consequences of drinking. People who want to manipulate you know how important your beliefs are in controlling your behavior. The next time you see a commercial, political speech, or other attempt to influence you, try to detect what belief they want you to accept and what behavior it is supposed to trigger. If you want to find out more about how people try to manipulate you, read about propaganda, techniques of advertising, and other ways of influencing behavior. You would find them both fascinating and useful.

Beliefs may be true or false. Just because we believe something does not make it true. Many of the beliefs we have had in the past have been found to be false. For example, not many years ago some people with white skin believed that people who had black, brown, or yellow skin were inferior or less than human. As a result, many of the non-white-skinned people were treated unfairly and inhumanely because of those beliefs. We now know these beliefs are not true, but they caused many people much grief.

On an individual level, some people (perhaps you?) believe they are not intelligent or capable even though they actually are quite capable. Because of this belief, they do not attempt to do things that they would like to do because they fear they will fail. They miss many opportunities in their lives because

353

they have the false belief that they are incapable. The point is that we act on our beliefs even when those beliefs are incorrect and people, even we ourselves, get hurt as a consequence.

The combination of a strongly held but incorrect belief can do a terrible amount of damage. History, and perhaps your personal experience, is full of examples of people who fanatically acted on their incorrect beliefs. Probably the most well-known example is the Nazi extermination of Jews in World War II. In Germany, it was widely and strongly believed that the Jewish people were responsible for the problems that Germans were having. This ultimately led to the extermination of millions of innocent men, women, and children simply because they were Jewish.

In the same way, there are individuals today (perhaps you?) who strongly believe they cannot control their addictions and behaviors, which are doing terrible physical and mental harm to them. Because they know (very strongly believe) that the world controls them and that they cannot control their own behaviors, they are unable to break out of their addictions. The addictions then rob them of their health, self-respect, productivity, freedom, and, in some cases, their lives. The strong acceptance of the belief that you are incapable of controlling your life is equivalent to sentencing yourself to a lifelong term in jail.

Sometimes we believe something so strongly that we feel compelled to force others to believe what we believe and behave as we behave. This is just another way of saying we believe that "my way is the best way" and everyone should do things my way. Attempts to convince others to "be like us" have resulted in the use of everything from subtle persuasion to full-scale wars.

Again, history is full of examples, but the easiest to see was during what we called the Cold War, in which the Communist nations, led by the U.S.S.R., and the democratic nations, led by the U.S., tried to convince the rest of the world they knew what was right. Both sides used drastic techniques of convincing others to adopt their correct beliefs. These included espionage, terrorism, assassinations, invasions, wars, and murders, as well as more subtle means such as propaganda, cultural exchanges, and various forms of aid.

There are less obvious examples of people forcing their beliefs on others all around us every day, however. It is happening in some families, schools, churches, governments, and businesses. Who has tried to force a belief on you lately? Have you tried to force a belief on someone else? Is it right to force a belief on someone no matter how good the belief is?

What people say they believe and how they act is not always consistent. If you want to be sure what someone believes, you will have to observe how he or she acts. People act consistently with their beliefs at the time of the action; however, what they say they believe may or may not be consistent with their actions.

Have you ever surprised yourself by acting in a way that was inconsistent with a belief that you had just thought about or expressed? If you go back to that situation and analyze it, you will find that you were acting consistently with another belief you hold, but it was not the same belief you had expressed just prior to the action.

Different beliefs can lead to disputes. Beliefs, especially strongly held ones, are the bases of arguments, disputes, clashes, and wars of all kinds. The next time you get into an argument, take note of the beliefs that are the foundation for the position taken by each side in the argument. If the beliefs are very strongly held and are not open to question, the chance of having a quick resolution (or any resolution) to the dispute is very small, and you could argue forever. If the beliefs are very different and irreconcilable, you may have to give up the futile discussion and simply agree to disagree.

Don't be afraid to question the beliefs you hold. Some people and some organizations never question their beliefs. Their beliefs become so rigid over time that no one thinks to question them. For example, most American families serve turkey for their Thanksgiving meals. They would be shocked if someone suggested that they have pizza or chow mein. In a more serious vein, some organizations are so rigid that they punish anyone who questions the organization's dogma or official set of beliefs. This is unfortunate because progress almost always begins with someone questioning beliefs, finding those beliefs to be unjustified, and then suggesting new beliefs that are more useful. For example, someone had to question the beliefs that the earth was flat, that women shouldn't be allowed to vote, and that it was moral to have human slaves.

Are you in situations such as relationships, family, work, or church in which you are not allowed to question established beliefs? Do you hold beliefs that you do not allow others to question? Do you hold beliefs that you will not question? You should not be afraid to question your beliefs. If you question a belief, there are three things that can happen. First, you might find that the belief stands up under the test and you hold it even stronger. Second, you might find that the belief needs to be modified to make it more useful in some way. And third, you might find that your belief is counterproductive to you or someone else and you should reject it. In each case, you are better off after you question your belief than before you questioned it, aren't you? There is nothing to fear.

Here are some beliefs that you might consider, adopt, question, discuss, modify, or reject:

- Respect is something you earn, not something you command or inherit by position or wealth.

- People should have opportunities to participate in making the rules by which they will have to live.

- People can learn just about anything if they see it as important and if they have enough time.

- It is immoral to drink and drive.

- Life is more enjoyable when you look for the positives in people and events.

- The world just is; we humans give it meaning.

- Emotions are human interpretations of emotionless events.

- You can find joy in the journey as well as the destination.

- There is no failure in our lives, only results or outcomes.

- The only stress in the world is in people's minds.

- Life is a miracle and should be treated that way.

- Physical activity is a major component of a healthy lifestyle.

- Ideas without action are no better than no ideas as at all.

- Common property (public property) should be treated as if it were your own property.

- Find joy in the small things and common things in life.

- It is better to strive for improvement rather than perfection.

- Catastrophes are almost always temporary inconveniences.

- You cannot expect more than one's best effort.

- Human consequences are the bottom line in making decisions.

- What you think about tends to come about or happen.

- Frogs can have fun, too.

QUESTIONS

1. What are your most strongly held beliefs? How did you obtain these beliefs?

2. Is there any belief that you would die for? Any that you would kill for?

3. What beliefs do you have about life, friendships, enemies, school, family, money, theft, killing, and death?

4. What do you believe constitutes a good life?

5. Did you ever find out that you had acted on an untrue belief? What happened?

6. Did anyone ever treat you badly because of an untrue belief that he or she had and then acted upon?

7. Do you have any beliefs that you feel everyone should have and act upon? Are those beliefs so valuable that you would advocate forcing others to adopt them?

8. Have you ever tried to force someone to believe in a certain way? Have you ever subtly tried to influence someone to believe a certain way?

9. Have you ever been in situations in which you knew someone else was trying to influence you to adopt one or more beliefs?

10. Do you believe you are mostly in control of your life or that you are mostly *not* in control of your life?

11. Can you think of examples of people believing one thing and doing another? Can you think of examples in your life in which you believed one thing and did another?

12. Can you think of any belief you hold that you would not question or allow anyone else to question? Why would you not question it?

13. Do you hold any beliefs of which you are not proud (i.e., you would not want others to know that you held them)?

ACTIVITIES

1. Take time to write down 25 honest beliefs you have about yourself. Now put a + (plus sign) by each one that is a positive belief about yourself. Next put a − (minus sign) by each one that is a negative belief about yourself. Did you learn anything about yourself and what you believe about yourself? Does this encourage any action on your part?

2. Have everyone in your group watch a different television show before the next meeting. As you watch the television show, note the beliefs that the show is teaching by the behavior of the characters in it. For example, a show in which disputes are always settled by a fight or a killing would be teaching the viewer that violence is the way to settle disagreements. Have everyone share their research with the others in the group. List everyone's findings. How many of the beliefs recorded would lead to positive human consequences if they were enacted? How many would you classify as leading to negative human consequences?

3. Follow the same procedure as in the previous activity but watch television commercials. What beliefs are the commercials attempting to get you to adopt? What actions are they attempting to get you to do?

4. Do you agree with the statement, "Progress almost always begins with someone questioning beliefs, finding those beliefs to be unjustified, and then suggesting new beliefs that are more useful"? Why or Why not? Can you give

examples from history or your own life of an instance in which this statement is true?

5. A list of beliefs appears at the end of the chapter. Which of these beliefs do you accept? Which ones do you not accept? Of the ones you do not accept, is there a way that you could modify the wording of the beliefs so that you could accept them?

6. Have everyone pretend that he or she could have the power to place two beliefs in everyone's brain in the world and that from then on, everyone in the world would act consistently with that belief. Write the beliefs in a place where everyone can see them and have each person explain the reasons for his or her choice.

7. Use some visual medium (such as a cartoon, painting, or drawing) to illustrate one of your beliefs.

8. Brainstorm about beliefs that you feel are really stupid, in that acting on the beliefs is ultimately harmful to people or the environment in some way. Explain each of the beliefs and the consequences of acting upon them.

CHAPTER 37

A Final Reminder

Hopefully, you have discovered that this book contains many useful ideas. Hopefully, you have chosen and used many of the ideas and have found that you have gained significantly more control over your life. You should be more productive, have more confidence in yourself, feel happier, be more optimistic about your future, and generally see your life as having improved.

If you have simply read through this book but have taken no actions to put the ideas into practice, however, you can't expect your life to change for the better. Don't be like those people sometimes called "self-help groupies" who go to all the seminars and workshops and read all the books but never take any action. Simply listening to a lecture, reading a book, or even participating in an intense workshop won't bring change in your life. A great idea not acted upon has the same results as never having the idea at all. Ultimately only *you* can bring about change in yourself. The motivation must come from within.

Because you have taken your valuable time to read this book, my guess is that you must have some desire to make changes in your life. This book gives many ideas about what you might want to change and how you might bring about that change. Now it is up to you to supply the effort to make your chosen lifestyle changes. You are a unique and fantastic "miracle" that has the opportunity, and perhaps the responsibility, to become even better.

Therefore, I again encourage and invite you to choose some of the ideas in this book and deliberately make them part of your lifestyle. If you feel content with your life at this point, you can choose not to accept the invitation or to accept it at a later time. If you feel, however, that you would like to make some changes in your life, you can accept this invitation to action and increase the probability that you can be more productive, self-confident, proud, and generally happier. It's up to you.

They are YOUR CHOICES and it is YOUR LIFE.